ENDORSEME

Christy Johnston is a true voice for this generation—a woman of conviction and a heart of purity to lead well. Her heart and tenacity for the family is contagious. She is a woman of the Word, and when she speaks the gates of hell tremble. *The Deborah Mantle* is a powerful read! As a woman, you will feel empowered by the Holy Spirit to lead well and live a life of boldness.

The Lord has been raising His Esthers and Deborahs in this hour to use their grace, beauty, purity, and roar for His glory. You will feel encouraged through the scriptures and personal storytelling of Christy's experiences of becoming the warrior God called her (and each one of us) to be. Get ready to be inspired to live a life of uncompromising faith.

Psalm 144:1 says, *"Blessed be the Lord my Rock, who trains my hands for war, and my fingers for battle."* (NKJV). Deborahs, it's your season to arise. It's the hour for the warriors to come forth. You may be a warrior in training, but by the time you finish reading this book you will be ready to pick up your sword. You were called by God for such a time as this. Every one of you is a lioness. It's time to release your roar!

Natasha Hinn

Blow the trumpet in Zion! Sound the alarm! *The Deborah Mantle* is a clarion call to a generation of women to cry loud, spare not, and take their position in battle. Each word carries authority, weight, and power. As a mother of three, this book has charged and awakened my spirit even more to run to the front lines and fight for the foundation of our nation and a generation. I am so thankful for Christy's *bold* stance on the demonic agenda of our day. It must be exposed for the light of His glory to invade the darkness and overturn every decree, plot, plan, and ploy of the enemy. We have been mantled and given a voice for such a time as this. Enough is enough. It's time! Sing, Deborah, *sing!*

JESSICA SCHLUETER
Worship pastor and young adults/youth pastor
Fresh Start Church

If ever there was an appointed time for the people of God to be empowered and equipped for battle, it is now! Christy Johnston doesn't play games when it comes to rallying women everywhere with a sense of urgency about walking out a very clear Kingdom assignment—no matter the season you are in.

Christy boldly and unapologetically unpacks divine strategy and insight into the times we are living in and does not hold back—by any means—when it comes to tackling current issues with biblical truth and prophetic wisdom, leaving no room for believers to abdicate responsibility when it comes to being a light in the darkness.

Filled to the brim with powerful revelation, a call to fervent prayer, and practical tools on how to dismantle and destroy the agenda of hell—this is not just a book, but an invitation to fearlessly partner with what God is doing all across the earth. It is not merely up to a select few to bring Kingdom solutions to the very real and controversial issues affecting the world today; it is up to believers everywhere to dare to be controversial enough to oppose the darkness and tear down the principalities that have set themselves up in every area of society. No more playing it safe, these pages will remind you once more of the unique voice and heaven-appointed authority that you have been given—and that both are needed now more than ever.

I cannot encourage every daughter, sister, mother, and wife enough to get your hands on this book and do not put it down until you catch *The Deborah Mantle!* It is time to arise!

Mia Fieldes
Songwriter

Women throughout biblical history have been given divine assignments. I believe God is calling women and mothers to stand fearlessly for truth to counter these times of mass deception. I'm encouraged by bold, God-fearing women like Christy Johnston and her powerful book, *The Deborah Mantle.* This book will inspire women to remember who they are and whose they are. May we declare truth boldly and fearlessly!

Landon Starbuck

There is a strategic frequency to the voice of women. I'm not referencing tone, pitch, high or low sounds; I'm talking about a spiritual frequency that has been gifted by God to speak His heart to generations. For too long that frequency has been fought and limited by the enemy. But God is raising up voices such as Christy Johnston to cry loud and spare not for the sake of families in our nations. In this book *The Deborah Mantle,* she will equip, challenge, and charge an army of women to release that unique frequency. There are principles and prophecies contained within these pages that will shift the trajectory of this generation. Read and speak, Deborah!

KIM OWENS
Author, *Doorkeepers of Revival* and
Just to Make Religion Mad
Co-pastor, Fresh Start Church
Peoria, Arizona

As a pro-life advocate, I spend a large amount of time counselling those who are recovering from an abortion. I've seen firsthand the need for igniting women of faith to take up the spiritual battle and use their God-given voices to help protect our most vulnerable. I've watched as Christy's mission to awaken and empower women has blossomed into a fierce call to action for us all to fill in the gap and embrace strong moral advocacy for our children. In this book, her prophetic voice ignites and prepares women to cloak themselves in the Deborah and Esther mantle. Packed with scripture, this book helps engage the hearts of God's daughters arming us all to action and cloaking us in God's strength.

TONI MCFADDEN
Pro-life advocate, international speaker, and author of
Redeemed: My Journey after Abortion

In our current church culture, a prophetic word is often speaking to the future, to a promise or a warning of things to come. But in the Old Testament, the prophets not only spoke of the future, but they spoke to the moment people were in. *The Deborah Mantle* is just that—a prophetic message that calls women to see the moment and engage. Christy powerfully reminds us of our calling as daughters of God and brings words of courage and hope. I highly recommend this book!

KIM WALKER-SMITH

Christy has tapped into the absolute sovereign Word of the Lord and the heart of the Father concerning this book! The mantle of Deborah is in fact upon us in a great measure, and she gives language to the Body of Christ to know the times and the seasons we are in. This book will stir you to a greater measure of prophetic revelation, insight, and fire!

JENNY WEAVER
Founder of The Core Group movement

Once again Christy has so poignantly and prophetically written a book that will equip and empower its readers to boldly arise and push back the darkness that has permeated our culture. Full of Kingdom perspective and strategy, *The Deborah Mantle* is essentially a call to be consecrated unto the Lord and respond to His invitation to courageously bring heaven to earth. This is a crucial, urgent, necessary message.

MEREDITH ANDREWS

"When village life had ceased, I, Deborah, arose a mother in Israel!" (see Judges 5:7). Like in days of old when Israel was being ravaged by enemies from every side, God is raising up warriors—women who have been anointed and appointed to do their part to bring victory to our land.

In her book, *The Deborah Mantle*, Christy Johnston has perfectly and powerfully articulated our world's current need for the qualities of Deborah to rise again in this hour.

Christy's writings are both timely and prophetic. A clear and urgent call to all who would be courageous enough to arise and take their place in this modern-day battle for the hearts and souls of this generation.

Leanne Matthesius

Christy Johnston has blessed the Body of Christ with a modern forerunner manual that will assist us to prepare the way of the Lord. As a mother who is passing a spiritual and cultural baton to my own ten children, I am grateful that Christy is training up a generation of mothers and daughters who understand that we must occupy until Christ returns.

ELIZABETH JOHNSTON
Mother of 10, bestselling author, speaker, podcast host, and pro-life activist

Christy is a voice for this generation.

Her intercession, pursuit of God, boldness, and spiritual fruitfulness are what I have been encouraged by for years. As usual, this book has come right on time— for this generation in history—because Christy reminds us of the importance of consecration in the secret place with the Lord. I believe this is the time to consecrate ourselves for holy, special purposes and to go all in to make ourselves ready for every good work.

The Lord prepared Deborah in the secret place, where she attuned herself to His voice. Her deep surrender, obedience and courage led all of Israel to a mighty victory over its oppressors. This book is a deep reminder to seek Him and His voice above all other voices...to love the praise and approval of God more than the praise and approval of man. Christy touches on some critical issues in our world today—all with a unifying, truth-filled Kingdom mindset but without the divisive polit-icized spirit. For instance, one of the lies of this generation is in the feministic movement that loudly resounds, "We have to fight for our identity!" However, the truth is found in the secret place with our Heavenly Father who tells us, "You find your identity in me, and you will fight FROM that identity!"

Faux Freedom, though, is running rampant, results in bondage, and literally leads in death. But where the Spirit of the Lord is, there is freedom—and I believe you will walk in greater freedom after reading this book.

I believe this book will be used to instill women's God-given identity back into their one true victorious, unshakeable identity in God. It will remind women who have fallen into fear or sleepy apathy to pick up their God-given authority and access to Him—which was paid for by the blood of Jesus—and walk in victory and fullness.

The enemy has pointed his sword at mothers and children for far too long because he is terrified of what this generation carries. But spoiler alert: The gates of Hell will never prevail.

This book is a reminder to pick up your Kingdom keys, to remember the victorious never-ending Kingdom of God, to start forbidding on earth what does not belong here and releas-ing Heaven into your daily lives.

May mothers arise and give themselves fully consecrated to Christ, to receive fresh vision of the arrows in their hands, to declare on earth as it is in Heaven in their marriages, children, homes and everywhere their feet go.

Courtney Smallbone
For King and Country

DESTINY IMAGE BOOKS
BY CHRISTY JOHNSTON

Releasing Prophetic Solutions

the
DEBORAH
MANTLE

A WOMAN'S CALL TO ARISE AND
SLAY THE GIANTS OF HER GENERATION

CHRISTY JOHNSTON

DESTINY IMAGE® PUBLISHERS, INC.

P.O. Box 310, Shippensburg, PA 17257-0310

"Promoting Inspired Lives."

This book and all other Destiny Image and Destiny Image Fiction books are available at Christian bookstores and distributors worldwide.

For more information on foreign distributors, call 717-532-3040.

Reach us on the Internet: www.destinyimage.com.

ISBN 13 TP: 978-0-7684-7227-1
ISBN 13 eBook: 978-0-7684-7228-8
ISBN 13 HC: 978-0-7684-7230-1
ISBN 13 LP: 978-0-7684-7229-5

For Worldwide Distribution, Printed in the U.S.A.

2 3 4 5 6 7 8 / 27 26 25 24 23

To every daughter who feels the stirring of a fierce courage arising within...
To my own daughters,
Charlotte, Sophie, and Ava, may you carry
this mantle all the days of your lives...
I pray each one of you who reads
these words will run with the
mantle of Deborah in this hour.
May you take down every giant that
stands in your way, all for His glory.

CONTENTS

FOREWORD

When the MeToo movement marched in DC—and in cities across the earth—I was deeply troubled. I knew that some of the vehement tenors of that march were justifiable because of the pain, oppression, and injustice inflicted upon women from the beginning of time. However, the collective bitterness and rage seemed to have been driven by a source beyond the natural realm. It was as if I could see the chariots of the goddess and hosts of darkness marching in the heavens above. Was it a heralding of the end-time eschatological movement of female rebellion—which is how Derek Prince understood the coming forth of the woman of wickedness as described in Zech 5:11—harsh bigoted words, or prophecy?

This I know, the MeToo leadership gang of five refused to allow pro-life feminists to speak on stage. The platform of rebellion demands the right to shed the innocent blood of the unborn under the guise of "My body. My choice!"

1

That movement took place immediately after a profound, prophetic encounter that we experienced in an Awaken the Dawn envisioning meeting in Virginia. About fifty of us were present when the Holy Spirit interrupted the agenda with a two-hour whirlwind of prophecy regarding the coming of a million women to the DC Mall to pray for America. It would be the last stand to save the nation! The revelation was that the gathering would be inspired by Psalm 68—Deborah's Psalm—describing Deborah's march to victory against the overwhelming armies of Sisera (Judges 4-5). The mobilization: *"The Lord gives the command; great is the company of the women who proclaim it,"* (Psalm 68:11).

Do you see it? A great showdown is upon us. The beautiful battling Bride of Christ—Deborah the prophetess and true mother in America—will arise in spiritual and ideological conflict against the false mother spirit who seeks to destroy women and her offspring—as seen in Revelation 12:1-5. This book, The Deborah Mantle, has been written by a true Aussie prophetess and mother who was transported to America by a word from God—it is a clarion call and biblical instructive war manual to the "Daughters of a New American Revolution!" Oh, but the book is more than words; there is a huge difference between giving a prophetic word and being the embodiment of that prophetic word.

Christy Johnston—like Deborah—is the loving and honoring WIFE of her husband Nate. She's a MOTHER of three beautiful children, a PROPHETESS, and a dreamer of dreams, who has groaned in deep seasons of fasting and travail. Christy has mobilized united prayer for revival and the ending of abortion and has challenged a school system's ideologies to protect her daughters—"Don't mess with my child!" She has stirred tens of thousands on her social media platforms with fearless challenges to the current cultural tide threatening to sweep away the West. She is wrapped in the mantle of Deborah and is now, through this book, throwing that mantle over an ever-increasing army of women warring for the soul of the nations alongside their Baraks.

"Village life ceased in Israel. It ceased to be until I arose; I, Deborah, arose as a mother in Israel. When new gods were chosen, then war came to the gates." (Judges 5:7-8 NKJV)

Not unlike the crisis in the days of Deborah, in 1973 with the ruling of Roe v. Wade, America chose new gods: the gods that our fathers did not know—the gods that demanded blood. War came to the gates! Fifty years later, God raised up a mother and judge who—like Deborah and like a modern-day Jael— brought the gavel down and drove the spike into the temple of Roe. Her name is Amy Coney Barrett—the United States Supreme Court Justice, who arose and became the swing vote ending Roe v. Wade. She may have saved a nation. Christy Johnston's strong voice—with a great host of women—was echoing in the earth the shattering sound of that gavel coming down.

In the sixties, once again, we chose new gods and war came to our city gates. The cultural revolution—fueled by the Vietnam War, student protests, the sexual and drug revolution, the generation divide, Berkeley, the Black Panthers, etc.—tore at the fabric and foundations of a nation. But once again Deborah arose, a true mother in America. I was made aware of one of our great Christian leaders who researched the history of revivals in America. He found that a prayer movement preceded every revival except one: the Jesus Movement of the 1970s, where tens of thousands of youth were saved. This man asked the Lord, "Why was there no prayer movement that preceded that great awakening?" The Lord answered, saying, "Oh, I had my prayer movement!" Churches were losing their kids to the rebellion of the 1960s. Millions were turning from the Lord and being swept into the godless lifestyles of the cultural upheaval. Then a mother arose—millions of moms fell to their knees and began to cry to the Lord in desperation for their lost and dying children. Suddenly, God answered their cries with a love and salvation song that has not been heard since. Shortly after the Beatles said, "We are more famous than Jesus," Jesus was on the front cover of Time magazine. God is the one who brings sudden reversals and sovereign comebacks called revivals. Never count Him out.

IT'S TIME again for Deborah to arise when the spiritual, cultural, sexual, and political crises in the nation reach far beyond the crises of our past. Esther must arise into the high places of government and education. Deborah must arise into leadership for law and justice, for adoption and foster care. Jael must drive the stake of truth into the destructive philosophies snaking even into our elementary schools. Businesswomen like Dorcas must fund the Jesus revolution. Lydia must be found turning her home into hubs of prayer. We are believing for 250,000 women prayer hubs where they would begin wrestling for their children, taking communion, and taking their place on the stage of history—they will be the first responders when Deborah calls for a million women on the Mall to gather in prayer.

Then I said to the nobles, the officials and the rest of the people, *"The work is extensive and spread out, and we are widely separated from each other along the wall. Wherever you hear the sound of the trumpet, join us there. Our God will fight for us!"* (Nehemiah 4:19-20 NIV).

Recently, Christy posted this quote by Charles Spurgeon: "I would rather speak five words out of the Bible than 50,000 words of the philosophers." This book in your hand is not just a rallying cry, it is an in-depth biblical word study of the story of Deborah. Immerse yourself in these words. The Bible clearly states, *"These things happened to them as examples and were written down as warnings for us, on whom the culmination of the ages has come"* (1 Corinthians 10:11 NIV). The writer of the book of Judges was careful to include the story of Deborah so that women and men who face the greatest rage against Christ and His followers, the greatest assaults against the truth, and persecutions with troubles at the end of the age, will be warned and rise up in unity, courage, and strategic spiritual warfare to overcome the powers of darkness. The writer of this book re-echoes once again the ancient theme and the ancient song of Deborah for such a time as this:

'Awake, awake, O Deborah! Awake, awake, sing a song! Arise, O Barak, and take hold of your captives, O son of Abinoam!' (Judges 5:12 BSB)

Lou Engle

INTRODUCTION

Can you feel it? The tension of the age, the growing resistance to God and all that is right and true. There is a war on your doorstep—it's not lingering in the distance, it's not in a foreign country, it has arrived at your door. Not a physical war filled with guns, machinery, and nuclear weapons. This war I speak of is a war of words and thoughts, a Trojan horse disguised to appear like a gift of love and acceptance. It is nothing more than an invasive army of destruction hidden behind cleverly articulated words designed to tear apart the very fabric of God's design of family and legacy. This is a war on the generations of tomorrow. You might not see any physical battle being waged at the threshold of your home, but if you were to peel back the curtain of the natural realm and see into the second heaven, you would see a vicious clash in the heavenlies. It is a spiritual conflict that you have been born into and are called to engage in. Can you feel it?

This war has been unleashed against the family—a war on our children, in which hell-inspired indoctrinations have been spreading and infiltrating schools, high schools, and universities. If the enemy hasn't been able to kill our children in the womb, he's been attempting to kill their image in Christ by way of their young minds. There is a remarkable anointing upon Generation Z and Generation Alpha to usher in a great outpouring of the Lord, and the enemy knows it. There has been an increased war against women—an attack on our wombs, the fruit of our wombs, and an attack against our God-given identity as daughters and mothers. We have ideologies being pushed that blur the lines between man and woman, and men are being told that masculinity is a modern-day evil. Human trafficking has increased and things like pedophilia, which was once considered evil, are being slowly accepted as an identity. Demon-filled theories are running rampant.

But God has an answer. Deborah. In Judges 5:7 (NKJV), the prophetess and judge Deborah sang these words as a prophetic war cry over her people: *"Village life ceased, it ceased in Israel, until I, Deborah, arose, arose a mother in Israel."* The New International Version puts it like this: *"Villagers in Israel would not fight; they held back until I, Deborah, arose, until I arose, a mother in Israel."*

The collision of light and darkness is evident all around. Maybe this war has caused you to question, "Is there any hope for my future and the future of my children?" The answer is a resounding *yes*. This is no call to fear, but a call to attention, for your name has been chosen for the front lines, daughter. You are being anointed to stand up and fight, and you are not alone—there is an army gathering upon the horizon. It is an army of God's daughters coming to claim their inheritance. I feel the ground shaking as they march together in unison, sending shock waves into the enemy's camp, for they come to retrieve their territory. I can see their eyes burning with a fierce passion for their Beloved; they are moving in response to His call. His call is one of urgency, like a drum beating with the sounds of war, whose notes are echoing out across the four corners of the earth. His voice calls out to His daughters: "Rise up, My daughters, rise up! I am releasing the mantles of Deborah and Esther to rest upon you in this hour. This is your moment. I am giving your enemies into your hands." In one hand, they carry the sword of the Spirit; in the other, they hold the Blood of the Lamb. They are moving to the sound of the Lion of the Tribe of Judah who is roaring behind them. They have come to rebuild the ancient ruins, to repair the cities destroyed, to revive and redeem the devastations of many generations.

Daughter, can you hear the call of the Beloved for the hour at hand? "Rise up, Deborah, and take the giants down."

Part One

THE DEBORAH CALL

Chapter One

THE VOICE CALLING OUT

You have to be near Him to hear Him.
—JARED BROCK

Following the Voice

On the tenth of March 2020, my husband Nate and I, along with our (then) two girls, left Australia for the United States on what would be one of the last flights out of our home country for almost two years. We didn't know this at the time, of course; otherwise, I doubt we would have left. We were obediently following the instructions of a dream that I was given in September of 2019. In that dream, I saw a calendar opened to March of 2020. The date of the tenth of March was circled in a big red marker, and every date after the tenth had a big black X over it. Before that dream, we had been in a five-year-long journey of preparing to move our family and set up our ministry in the United States following a multitude of prophetic words; however, our long-term visas were still in process at this point. Given that there was no finalization yet, we instinctively knew that this was a directional dream to plan a trip to the United States. Our plans were to leave on the tenth of March for a three-month journey on a temporary visa to scout out the land. We booked our return flights and were due to fly home to Australia in June of 2020, in the hopes that our permanent visas would be finalized by then, so that we could go to our interview with the U.S Consulate in Sydney and hopefully return later that year. (Sounds confusing, I know.) At least, that was what we thought would happen.

That one dream continues to astound me to this day, because as I look back upon it, a domino effect took place simply because we followed the voice of God. If we had not followed His direction because it seemed as though things in the natural had not yet lined up, a domino chain of events would not have taken place. I love what Lou Engle says about dreams:

> We say it was "Just a dream." What do you mean "just a dream"? Who knows what angels had to fight through to break into your world to give you their thoughts and you just say, "It's just a dream"? I think the church needs to stop saying, "It's just a dream."

How many dreams have you written off as "just a dream" when it was the voice of God giving you heavenly coordinates, divine timing, and instruction? I encourage you, pay attention to your dreams, because they are often warnings, instructions, and directions from the Lord.

Boarding our flight on the tenth of March 2020 was a bizarre experience. You must remember, when I had had this dream in September of 2019 news of COVID-19 was yet to break into the world domain. By the time we left in March, the pandemic had reached the height of fear as panic swept across the earth and held a global audience spellbound. News of this virus spreading into every country had rapidly increased by the day and the headlines out of Australia had caused mass panic and upheaval—so much so that we were being told to cancel travel plans and hunker down. Despite this, we just knew we had to follow the voice of God in the dream. The airport was the quietest I had ever seen it, and I could feel the presence of an eerie fog filled with terror invading every square inch of the atmosphere. People were acting erratically, and I had never seen the public so afraid to talk to one another until now. Even the customs officers were more harsh, distant, and abrupt than usual. It was a disturbing feeling to be leaving the comfort and safety of home during what felt like a worldwide war zone. As we settled into our seats on our plane, preparing for takeoff to San Francisco, panic and grief began to wash over me like a flood. I looked at our two little girls sitting next to me, headsets on, settled in contentedly watching a movie with their snack boxes in their laps that I had packed for them earlier, blissfully unaware of the hysteria that surrounded them, and I couldn't help but feel the uncertainty of what we were doing.

I looked over at Nate, sitting in the aisle seat opposite me, as tears poured down my face, and he knew exactly what I was thinking: *Have we missed it? Are we doing the right thing? Are we putting our children in danger?* He looked at me assuredly and mouthed the words to me, "Trust Him!" As we turned onto the runway with the engines beginning to roar and we accelerated for takeoff, I felt the presence of the Holy Spirit rest upon me like a blanket just as I felt the gravitational force of takeoff. I could hear the whisper of His voice above the noise of the engines, and as the wheels of our plane lifted off the ground, I heard Him say, "I am with you."

Tears continued to stream down my face, and despite the fear, I whispered back, "I trust You. I'm following You."

We would be one of the last flights leaving Australia, and one of the last Australian flights landing in the United States for over two years. Days later, the borders of our country would be locked down, and our returning flights would be cancelled. As the dream had revealed, March 10 was circled, and every date thereafter was crossed off. It wouldn't be until months later that we would recognize the impact this one act of obedience would have upon our lives. We thought we would be back in just a few short months, but we wouldn't return for 20 long months.

Are you in a place right now where you are feeling the pressing fear of culture around you? It may no longer be a natural virus that's concerning you, but a plague of deception and godlessness that's now invading hearts and minds all over the earth.

Are you seeing this rising trend of opposition to God that is causing you to fear the future? Are you wondering, "Have I missed it? Are my children or my family in danger?" I have a promise for you today: "She is clothed with strength and honor, and she laughs without fear of the future" (see Proverbs 31:25).

This is the Father's promise over you, daughter. You are one who is clothed in strength and honor. These two words in this verse illustrate a spiritual clothing, like royal robes adorning your shoulders. Strength and honor speak of your spiritual authority. It is the strength of the Father that will carry you. The word *honor* can be translated into "glory," for it is His glory that will illuminate the darkness. You do not have to fear the future, for there are spiritual anointings and tools He has given you to walk into the days ahead with joy and delight. We are on a spiritual runway right now, about to accelerate into a higher realm, another dimension, where the Spirit of the Lord is longing to pour Himself out like never before upon those who will listen. He is looking for a people who, through their own fears and tears, will cry out, "I trust You. I don't know what this is going to look like, but I trust You."

Are you listening? Are you willing to lean into the whisper of His voice above the noise of all that surrounds you? Are you ready to go where He leads? He's looking for those He can rest His anointing upon, and in this hour I sense He is longing to cloak a company of His daughters with the mantle of Deborah—a mantle that invokes insight, courage, and victory. Daughter, it's you He is looking to anoint. All that's required of you is to say, "Here I am, Lord. I trust You."

Whose Voice Are You Listening To?

You may have picked up this book out of curiosity, wondering, *What exactly is the mantle of Deborah?* Perhaps you have had prophetic words spoken over you regarding Deborah, or you simply love her story in the Bible. Regardless of what brought you here, I want to tell you that you belong here. Your voice matters here, and I believe it is no coincidence that you are right here in this moment, reading these words, because the Holy Spirit has led you here. He is anointing you with the mantle of Deborah in this hour because what you carry is crucial to fulfilling what He longs to pour out upon the earth in these last days.

So what is the mantle of Deborah, you may ask? Let's find out. We first find Deborah in Judges 4, but her story really begins in chapters 1–3 of Judges. A study of the first three chapters of Judges will take you into a culture of rebellion akin to the culture that surrounds us today. These first chapters will lead you on a tumultuous ride of ups and downs filled with disobedience and failure on the part of God's people. The Israelites continually did evil in the sight of the Lord, and in a moment of time when they were called to be taking territory and driving out their enemies, they instead partnered with them, lived among them, and built altars alongside them. They failed miserably to follow what God had asked of them, which was to drive out their enemies and destroy their altars. I wonder, did the Israelites think it unloving to drive out their enemies as God had directed? What caused them to completely turn aside from God's clear instruction to drive out *all* the Canaanites? Did they perhaps feel God's instruction was a little too harsh?

In Judges 1:27-34, we read an account of their failure to complete the conquest. In verse after verse, we discover how Israel's tribes failed to drive out the Canaanites. The Hebrew name *Canaan*, read *kena'an*, is derived from the root כנע (*kena*) meaning "to be brought down by a heavy load." It's no coincidence that the chaotic journey that the Israelites endured through the first chapters of Judges is because they failed to pursue their enemies before them. By partnering with them, they were brought down by a heavy and burdensome load. To give you some perspective, let's read Judges 1:27-29 (ESV) together:

> *Manasseh did not drive out the inhabitants of Beth-shean and its villages, or Taanach and its villages, or the inhabitants of Dor and its villages, or the inhabitants of Ibleam and its villages, or the inhabitants of Megiddo and its villages, for the Canaanites persisted in dwelling in that land. When Israel grew strong, they put the Canaanites to forced labor, but did not drive them out completely. And Ephraim did not drive out the Canaanites who lived in Gezer, so the Canaanites lived in Gezer among them.*

Manasseh failed to do what would ensure peace and freedom for their people for generations to come. Interestingly, some 700 years later Israel installed a king by the same name who followed in the same footsteps. Allow me to show you how. Manasseh was the king of Judah during 687-643 BC, and his name gives us a clue to what he was anointed to fulfill during his reign. His name means, "God has made me entirely forget my troubles." Names in biblical history were given to speak of the calling of God upon their lives, and it is evident that Manasseh was appointed to drive out the forces of darkness before him, which would lead the people into a habitation where they would forget their troubles. Instead, he failed to do so. He permitted their enemies to dwell among them, shunning his responsibility. The reputation of his reign became the opposite of what God intended for him—he yielded to idols, led the Israelites astray, and left the people vulnerable to the enemies within.

This leads us to the meanings of the enemy inhabitants that Manasseh permitted to remain. Collectively, their names mean "a wandering invasion of troops that devours the people in the habitation of tranquility." God's design for His people is to dwell in tranquility, but when we permit enemies to dwell within our midst, we allow a wandering invasion of troops that will devour the people. The tribe of Ephraim too was destined to drive out the enemies before them, and their name also speaks of the promise of God upon their life to do so. Their name means "fruitful." They were called to produce fruitfulness in their conquest. Instead, they permitted their enemies to dwell among them in Gezer, which means "a dividing sentence." In Judges 2:1-5 (ESV) the Lord sent His angel to deliver this message to the Israelites:

> *And he said, "I brought you up from Egypt and brought you into the land that I swore to give to your fathers. I said, 'I will never break my covenant with you, and you shall make no covenant*

*with the inhabitants of this land; you shall break
down their altars.' But you have not obeyed my
voice. What is this you have done? So now I say, I
will not drive them out before you, but they shall
become thorns in your sides, and their gods shall
be a snare to you." As soon as the angel of the Lord
spoke these words to all the people of Israel, the
people lifted up their voices and wept. And they
called the name of that place Bochim. And they
sacrificed there to the Lord.*

These words stand out to me: *"you have not obeyed my voice."*
The Hebrew word for *voice* is the word *qol*, and in *Strong's Concordance* (which, by the way, we will use a lot throughout this book to explain deeper meanings in scripture) *qol* is described as a loud outcry, a roaring sound, growling, crying, and a voice like the sound of a thunderbolt, among other definitions. This tells us that God was not quiet in His instruction to His people, and yet still His people refused to listen to His voice and follow His direction, even when they possibly thought His sentence was too harsh or didn't make sense. It's amazing that their neglect to listen to His voice resulted in the weeping of their own voices. For this word, *qol*, also means weeping and wailing. This is also the definition of *Bochim*, the place where they sacrificed to the Lord upon recognition of their failure. When we don't follow the voice of God, it will eventually lead us into a humbling place of weeping conviction and repentance.

Is it possible that we are seeing a similar story unfold before our own eyes in today's world? I don't know about you, but I feel we are in this place of Bochim right now. God has called us, His people, to drive out the forces of darkness in our own lands and territories. Instead of following His voice, we have feared the voice of the enemy above His and allowed a darkness to dwell among us. We have accepted destructive ideologies in the name of love and have tolerated the enemy's plans rather than confronting them. Our enemy may not be a physical army of troops (and I pray we will never have to face a physical war), but in many ways our enemy and the war we face is an invisible one, a wandering army of thoughts—an invasion of ideologies that have devoured the people and divided our habitations of tranquility. By not confronting these demons of thought when they were in their infancy, we have permitted a dividing sentence upon the people. Division has invaded the hearts and minds of the world. Perhaps you have noticed a trend in these divisive doctrines. Schools of thought that are cleverly voiced by the enemy to deconstruct God's original design are captivating this generation. The enemy cannot create; he can only imitate and divide. Today, we have armies of thought invading the creation of God in every aspect of His design. From the godless belief that the child in the womb is not human or worthy of protection, to the acceptance and even glorification of gender dysphoria. The voice of the enemy has grown loud.

King David wrote of the voice of the enemy using this same word, *qol*, and his response to the sound of the enemy's noise was one we can learn from in this hour. He said in Psalm 55:2-7 (NKJV):

> *Attend to me, and hear me; I am restless in my*
> *complaint, and moan noisily, because of the*

voice of the enemy, because of the oppression of the wicked; for they bring down trouble upon me, and in wrath they hate me. My heart is severely pained within me, and the terrors of death have fallen upon me. Fearfulness and trembling have come upon me, and horror has overwhelmed me. So I said, "Oh, that I had wings like a dove! I would fly away and be at rest. Indeed, I would wander far off, and remain in the wilderness."

Did you notice the voice of the enemy was drowning out the voice of the Father for David in these verses? David said, "I am distraught at the voice of the enemy." I want you to take a moment to reread these verses and consider the effect the voice of the enemy had on David. Rather than making God bigger than his situation, he made the voice of the enemy louder than anything else, which caused him to want to retreat. Fear and trembling gripped him. Does that sound anything like today to you?

Ever since 2020 arrived, fear and trembling has gripped the earth, sound reason has flown out the window, and insanity has instead prevailed over many. Take note of this tactic, because I want you to familiarize yourself with the voice of God again, if you haven't already. It is the voice of God that first calls you; it is His voice that anoints you and equips you for the hour at hand. Just as it was God's voice that birthed creation, it was His voice that communed with Adam in the garden. Yet in a moment of destiny like this one, the enemy will use the only tool in his arsenal that he has, and it's his own voice interlaced with lies. His methods have not changed since Eden. He has no weapons other than his voice, so he will use the whisperings of his voice to pressure you into fear or apathy, which leads to stagnation. If satan can't stop God from anointing you in this hour with the mantle of Deborah, threatened as he is by what this mantle means for him, he will attempt to lull you into a state of sluggish fear and inaction.

This idleness always follows the voice of intimidation. He will whisper to you through the enormity of the evil that surrounds you and begin to have you question your role in it all. "Who do you think you are?" he will whisper. "Do you really think you have what it takes to change all of this? Are you sure God called you to this?" Just as he did with Adam and Eve when he questioned *the* Voice, he will do with you. I want you alert to this strategy as you read through this book. As you come to learn the revelation of what the mantle of Deborah truly is, the voice of the enemy will try to convince you that you are not ready. I'm here to tell you today, you are.

Amazingly, *qol* can also be translated to mean all of the following: "news, noise, outcry, proclamation, public, report, screamed, shout." I want to highlight a few of these definitions, particularly *news, noise, outcry, public, report*. Does this sound familiar? The voice of the enemy often comes through the sound of the news. Notice how "noisy" your social media newsfeeds are. Notice the public outcries and shouts against anyone who stands for righteousness. Notice the reporting that roars loudly against those speaking the truth. Does "cancel culture" sound familiar in these definitions? It is the *qol* of the enemy—a public outcry because of news and noise. *Qol* is also the same word used to describe the voice of God in the Garden of Eden. However, there is a strategic context in this word that I want you to see. In Genesis 3:8, we find Adam and Eve hiding from God. They had just committed the first sin after listening to the voice of the enemy, and now they hear the *voice* of the Lord looking for them.

> *And they heard the voice of the Lord God walking in the garden in the cool of the day: and Adam and his wife hid themselves from the presence of the Lord God amongst the trees of the garden* (Genesis 3:8 KJV).

"They heard the *voice* of the Lord God." Notice that the voice of God sounds different when it is perceived through the voice of the enemy. Adam and Eve were hiding from the Lord because they were afraid of Him. Why? They had listened to the voice of the serpent—the noise, report, and sound of the enemy was louder in their ears than the true voice of their Creator. Now, through the muffled distortion of sin, God's voice suddenly sounded terrifying, not reassuring. Had they recognized the difference in voices to begin with, perhaps they never would have eaten the fruit, but because they questioned the voice of the Lord, His voice was no longer a comfort *but a threat*.

Interestingly, we have a world today responding to the voice of God in the same way. Truth is perceived as a threat and lies are perceived as love, all because the world has questioned the voice of their Creator, God. Pay close attention to this tactic of the enemy in the way he used his voice in the

Garden of Eden, for his tactics remain the same today. He said to Eve, "Did God really say?" Under this guise of questioning, God's voice is perceived as a threat. However, the Lord has released an antidote into this generation that will drown out the noise and the public outcry provoked by the enemy, and it is the song of Deborah and Barak. The mantle of Deborah is more than just an anointing that will rest upon one person; it is a mantle that the Lord is causing to rest upon an entire generation of laid-down daughters who are in love with their King.

Are you feeling the restlessness David spoke of? Is there a frustration you are sensing deep in your spirit that you just can't shake? Are you seeing the daily swirls of news and it is causing an agitation in the depths of your soul that you just can't move from? This restlessness is similar to the feeling a mother gets in the days leading up to the birth of her child. Her tummy is full; there is no more room left for growth; this baby must come out one way or another. If you are feeling this, it means the Lord is indeed calling you to this mantle, which also means you are being equipped for it. God did not design a woman with the ability to grow a baby without the capacity to birth the baby. In the same way, you are being adorned with this mantle. He is anointing you and fashioning you with the tools you will need to walk in it. I know without a shadow of a doubt that this book is in your hands for a reason. You, daughter, are called to this mantle. God will often allow you to feel the vast disparity between what should be and what is, because He is looking to awaken you to this anointing. He has called you to fill that void; He has called you to prophesy the difference. He will permit the agitation within your spirit to awaken you to the battle around you. Ultimately, this is an invitation into victory, but as the saying goes, "There is no victory without first a battle."

I do have a gentle warning for you in this—the unrest within you will only continue to grow until you respond. The more you try to run from it, the more it will increase. This is a holy disquiet; it is the wrestle of the Holy Spirit within your own spirit that is calling you higher into this appointment of destiny. It's His voice that tethers your heart to His, calling you, inviting you, and summoning you to answer the call and receive the anointing of the mantle of Deborah for the generations around you. If that feels a little daunting, I don't want you to close the book and make like an ostrich, diving your head in the sand. (Trust me, I've had many of those moments when I've longed to do just that.) I believe you have picked up this book because the Lord wants to fill your arsenal with the tools you will need for the days ahead. In the same way He has divinely designed the body of a woman to carry and birth new life, He has designed and equipped His daughters to carry and birth supernatural new life. I hear Him saying to you today, "You are not alone, I am with you, and I have strengthened you for this hour at hand. I have called you to this moment of time because I have given you what you need to bring about My victory."

Awake, Awake, Deborah

In Judges 5, we find one of my favorite portions of scripture—the song of Deborah and Barak. This may be jumping to the end of the story here before we have even begun, but I want you to see the significance of verse 12 before we move on.

> *Awake, awake, Deborah! Awake, awake, break out in a song! Arise, Barak, lead away your captives, O son of Abinoam* (Judges 5:12 ESV).

The Hebrew word for *song* is *dabar*, which means "to speak, assert, boast, command, counseled, directed, declare, passed sentence, preach, proclaim, repeated, spoken, said, sing, speak fluently, statement, subdue, threaten, utter."

God's remedy for the toxicity of satan's lying voice in the atmosphere of culture is His voice spoken through *you*, His daughters. But I want you to notice the profound difference in the meanings of the words in this song where they also speak of the voice. This song tells a much different story. The words *counseled, directed, repeated, and were spoken.* These give us a hint into the victory that God is longing to take you into, and it all starts with following His voice. Deborah and Barak were counseled and directed by the voice of God into battle, as a result, they repeated what He spoke, and His song became their song. Barak's name amazingly means "lightning strike." I find that profound given one of the meanings of the Hebrew word *voice, qol,* is defined as a thunderbolt. God's voice counteracts and strikes the voice of the enemy. I strongly believe the Holy Spirit is looking for a company of daughters and sons alike who are committed to repeat what He says, to sing what He sings, and to declare and utter *His* voice into an atmosphere filled with lies. He is looking for you, daughter, to dismantle the lies spoken over a generation and to declare the truth of who He has called them to be. When your ears are attuned to His voice, you walk in authority to set the captives free. You proclaim the promise and *repeat* what God has said until it breaks the mind-blinding spirits off this generation.

It's the roaring voice of God speaking fluently through you that will *subdue* the enemy under your feet. It's the growling voice of God that *threatens* the enemy as you utter the name of the King of kings, Jesus. Daughter, this is your hour to awaken, to break out in song and lead the captives out of captivity, to bring the prodigals home and point them to Jesus. Deborah's mantle is an anointing of courage; it sets her apart from the tribe of Manasseh, who simply permitted the existence of invading enemies. Her anointing is to rightly divide the word of truth and execute justice on behalf of God's people. It requires her to be sitting in the presence of the Lord and receiving His instruction. She doesn't stand alone; she partners with others to bring about the fulfilment of victory. She charges onto the battlefield unafraid, and in a time when everyone else is retreating, she is advancing. She doesn't sit idly by while the culture around her crumbles; she engages with the realm of heaven and stirs armies to attention, leading and guiding them down the mountain into a direct assault on the enemy's camp. She tears down the altars and raises up the banner of righteousness for the sake of her children, her family, and her nation. The Deborah mantle resembles that of John the Baptist, whose mission was to prepare the way of the Lord. Hers is an anointing that cries out, "Make way, prepare the way of the Lord," as she drives out the demon forces of wickedness and makes straight the path of the King.

This, daughter, is the hour to which you have been called, and you are being anointed with the Deborah mantle. Are you awake? Are you ready?

Deborah's Arsenal

I encourage you to take a moment to read through this reflection of Deborah's weapons that I have provided for you at the end of each chapter. Grab your journal and write down notes; take the time to allow these keys to sink deep into your spirit. These are keys taken directly from her story that will equip you as you carry this mantle.

Weapon #1: The Voice

Deborah was a prophetess, which means she was in tune with the prophetic voice of the Lord. Prophecy is voicing the Lord's intentions, thoughts, plans, warnings, and solutions over the future ahead of time. This mantle of Deborah is a prophetic mantle. It's imperative, therefore, that you are correctly hearing God's voice and giving voice to His thoughts—not the enemy's. You will know it's the voice of the Lord because His voice carries strategy, purpose, and hope. Attune your ears to what He is saying and proclaim His Word that is alive, powerful, and active and release His voice over the lies. Like arrows released from your mouth are your prophetic decrees of His goodness and His hope and His purpose. Release them—bull's-eye.

The Charge: Prophesy His Heart over the Problem

Ask yourself, "Whose voice have I been listening to? Is the voice of the enemy drowning out the voice of God in my life?"

If you answered yes to that question, take a moment to open up the scriptures. If you don't know where to turn, open up Psalms and spend some time reading until a verse of hope and purpose jumps out at you. When you find that verse, I want you to write it down in a journal. Rehearse the promise; speak it out daily.

God's promises are not whimsical, wishful thinking. They are like an anchor that pulls the reality of heaven into our reality here on earth. The anchor of His promise keeps the vessel of your heart securely stationed in heaven's reality. You may be surrounded by the storms of the enemy's plans, with furious waves lapping up over the hull of your mind, tempting to lash you with fear, but God's promises will keep you fixed on Him until the storm calms and His words manifest in your reality. Whenever fear arises in your heart, run to that promise, and declare it over the lies—let them be an anchor that holds His promises down deep in your heart.

Where have you been believing lies the most?

Reflect on where these lies are coming in. Are they thoughts of hopelessness about your future? Are they fears for your children's future? Do these lies reflect the reports of the news? If so, it's time to get a new report. Find your weapons in God's Word, in the spoken decrees of what He has said, and wage war with them—shouting them, declaring them, announcing them, and rehearsing them over the lies. If you do this, you *will* see the deliverance of the Lord in your life as a result.

Chapter Two

VILLAGE LIFE CEASED UNTIL

*May it never be said of me that I was
silent in the face of fear, and in so doing
passed on the battle to my children.*
—Christy Johnston

I was rocking my baby to sleep. Just months old, she was snuggled up like a tiny football on my chest with her head resting upon my shoulder as I slowly paced up and down the room. She was finally settling after a morning of fussiness. This being my third baby, I wasn't in a rush, intentionally embracing every moment of baby life, even the difficult moments, knowing just how fleeting that time is. As I gently patted her back, swaying back and forth and watching her eyelids droop, my gaze turned outside.

Our bedroom at the time was overlooking a spring land-scape of blossoming trees, and I could just see the melting snow-capped peaks of Mount Lassen in the near distance. We had been living in Redding, a town in northern California, for almost a year now (all from following that initial dream in March of 2020), and those mountain views never grew old, always alluring and drawing me into prayer. Nature does that for me; I find it to be an invitation to talk to the One whose hands formed it all—our Creator. So as I continued to gaze at the snowy mountain and sway, I began talking to the Lord when, suddenly, I felt a sick feeling forming in the pit of my stomach.

Ava had been born in January of 2021, a time of extreme tumult in the United States, and by April it was no different. I suddenly felt my emotions being swept out of this tender moment with her and the Lord as my mind began to race with reminders of the chaos that surrounded us in the world. My thoughts were filled with worst-case scenarios. It wasn't just the political upheaval; it was the constant news cycle of change, crisis, governmental heavy-handedness, and restrictions, all mixed with this thought: *We're never going back to normal* following the COVID crisis. I held this sweet little baby in my arms and wondered quietly to the Lord, *Will she ever know the world we knew before now? Will she ever know the freedom of traveling as we once did as a family? Will she ever be able to meet our family back in Australia? Will she have any kind of future?* My spirit was grieving, and fear was trying to grip my heart into hopelessness.

Perhaps you're reading this 20 years from the time I am writing, and you already know the other side of our future.

However, in that moment of time, it truly felt that things would never return to any kind of normalcy, let alone a future filled with hope for my children. There was endless talk of intense restrictions, limitations, and freedoms being taken away. However, it was also the ongoing barrage of exposure—all kinds of evil were being brought into the light, and it was weighing heavy on my heart and mind as well. During all this political and cultural shaking, ideologies were also swirling and still are to this day. Unchangeable truths were being brought into the public square of social media and mocked mercilessly.

We have known these things would come. Scripture warned us of these days we are now living. Romans 1:25 (NIV) foretold us, "*They exchanged the truth about God for a lie, and worshiped and served created things rather than the Creator—who is forever praised. Amen.*" Yet the warning of this reality taking place did not make things any easier for me, especially as I was holding this defenseless newborn. There was also the threat of the growing agitation against Christianity swirling in my mind, and even the struggles within our own Christian family of brothers and sisters in Christ. It felt like a tug of war in which we watched fellow brothers and sisters fall to the whims of worldly doctrines, which was particularly difficult for my heart and mind to comprehend. Since the Holy Spirit led us into full-time ministry in 2016, Nate and I have led thousands of students through our online community and school called Grow. We have witnessed God move in countless lives through this little idea that God gave me in August of 2016 to lead others into growth in their relationship with Jesus. Our hearts were to launch others into their own destinies, to be their cheerleaders where we felt we had none, and it has been our greatest joy to lead.

The year 2020 arrived like an earthquake, and the year that followed was like the aftershocks. We were also being tested in our leadership. As any other minister in the Body of Christ could testify, those two initial years tested us all in our foundations. How would we respond to certain issues? How would we lead through the storms? Would we find ourselves shaken, or would we dig ourselves deeper into our root system of Christ? While I know we made mistakes and didn't do things perfectly, I can say with clear conviction that I know those shakings only further anchored our faith in Jesus and His Word. Add to all of this, pregnancy and a new baby, all while being forcefully isolated from family due to the lockdowns, and you can understand my feelings of anxiety. Every facet of life felt shaky, and I think I can assume that we were all feeling it, learning, perhaps for the first time—and if not for the first time, at least in a new way—what it meant to be firmly planted on the Rock. Maybe you can relate to this bewilderment and overwhelming feeling I speak of. The rapid rate at which life, culture, ideologies, and chaos have increased since 2020 is unlike anything any of us have experienced in recent history.

As I gazed outside and beyond to the mountain before me, I felt as though I was standing directly in front of that mountain and it was towering—not beautifully, as it naturally appeared, but menacingly above me, taunting me, mocking me with thoughts of anguish, especially over the future of my children and their generation. I broke down quietly in tears so as not to wake my now-settled baby. It was then, with tears streaming down my face, that I felt a gentle nudge from the Holy Spirit. "Ask Me what I'm thinking," I heard Him say.

So I asked, "What do You say to this mountain? What are Your plans for my children? What do You say about everything that is swirling right now?"

Right then, as though He was standing there with me, looking out at the mountain together, with His hand on my shoulder, I heard His whisper: "Christy, you don't need to fear tomorrow. You're raising the future of tomorrow in your arms. Tomorrow fears you." I broke down again, this time in relief, realizing that it was the Father and I together who determine what tomorrow will look like for my children and my children's children. Not the enemy.

Perhaps today, in many ways you are feeling the same as I did in that moment. Is fear gripping you as you look at the shaking of worldly systems and the clashing of ideologies? Are you wondering what kind of future your children or grandchildren will have? I know there are many who are reading this book too who don't have physical children, but maybe you are wondering, *Where does hope fit into it all?* Do you feel weighed down by grief from the increase of evil? Are you seeing and feeling the taunts of the wicked pressing in on all sides of culture and life? Is the daily assault on truth and the Gospel overwhelming you? It may appear that village life is ceasing all around. The culture as you knew it and the sense of security found in familiar truths and realities mixed with old habitual comforts may be crumbling all around. I want to encourage you with this same message from the Father, "You don't have to fear tomorrow—tomorrow fears you." The question is not,

"Will your children have a future?" The question is, "Will you pass on the battles of today into their futures tomorrow?"

Cultural Metamorphosis

When my daughter Charlotte was just five years old, I was in the process of enrolling her into a public school that had a wonderful reputation in our area. I was at the very end of the enrolment process when I had a check in my spirit to ask about a program that was cunningly named "Safe Schools." This program had been recently introduced into Australian schools across the nation, though not every school had yet adopted it into their curriculum. This eight million dollar program, federally funded by our Australian government, was a façade of safety, but hidden deceptively behind it's comforting name was a pit of grotesque gender ideologies and sexualized content being taught to children as young as six, encouraging young girls to bind their chests and young boys to wear dresses. It was anything but safe.

I was so happy with every other detail about this school—the teachers were lovely, the school was in a beautiful location surrounded by Australian bushland, the education they offered was wonderful, with a range of different extracurricular activities. I was ready to go ahead and sign the paperwork, except for this niggle in my spirit that told me otherwise. Nowhere in any of the enrollment forms did I find information or parental consent about this program, so I had assumed that it had not yet been introduced by this particular school. Yet I couldn't ignore the urge in my spirit that I needed to ask further. If I had not listened to that all-familiar prompting of the Holy Spirit, I likely wouldn't have ever known it was being taught to my daughter until, perhaps, the damage had been done. It was only because I had known of this program's existence that I decided to arrange an appointment with the principal to ensure it was not being taught at this school.

During our appointment, the principal led me outside to sit under the violet umbrella of a Jacaranda tree while Charlotte played on the playground equipment close by. "We're very excited to welcome you," she started out.

"We are excited too," I replied. "I just wanted to ask about a program I have heard about and wanted to know if it has been introduced here—a program called Safe Schools," I queried.

The principal's eyes lit up in delight as she began telling me how proud she was to be one of the first schools in our state of Queensland to introduce it. My heart sank. I had been doing some of my own research about the program itself and what I had found was extremely alarming. However, I wanted to address some of my concerns with her directly. "I've heard that parents aren't even notified of their children being taught this program. Is this true? Do you ask for our permission to teach this content?"

She stumbled, "Well, not exactly."

I questioned further, "Well, what is it precisely? Are you teaching young boys and girls that their gender is fluid?"

"Oh yes, of course," she replied, not yet cluing on to my growing agitation. She continued, "We already have one child in our classes who was born in a boy's body but identifies as a girl. In fact, 'she' will be in your daughter's class. It's a wonderful way to teach acceptance," she finished, triumphantly.

I looked at her sternly, making my position clear as I emphasized his male biology: "And will this boy be in the same bathrooms as my daughter? How about when they are changing for swimming classes? Will he be in there with all the little girls?"

Finally understanding my opposition, the principal grew flustered. "Why yes, she will participate in every girl activity because she is a girl!" She was bitterly exasperated.

"You and I have a problem," I added. "You evidently believe that affirming gender confusion in a five-year-old child, who can't even yet tie their own shoelaces properly, is somehow a step forward in our society. I call that foolishness. The problem you are subjecting these children to, based on acceptance, is a lifetime of identity crisis, and I would define that as child abuse. I will have nothing to do with a school that puts my daughter into a predicament where she must share a bathroom with a boy, let alone getting changed in front of him and vice versa. I won't be enrolling my daughter into your school after all." I immediately grabbed the paperwork out of her hands, called for Charlotte and walked away, leaving the principal aghast, her jaw dropped in a look of shock and disgust at my confrontation.

Today, some six years on, I have only seen this indoctrination of gender ideologies grow more rapidly. To quote a journalist, "The speed with which modern society has adapted to accommodate the world's vast spectrum of gender and sexual identities may be the most important cultural metamorphosis of our time," wrote Jenna Wortham in *The New York Times*.[1] I want you to think on what Jenna is truly saying here. The swift upending of a foundational truth like the biological gender you were born with, the identity God created you in, is an apparent "important cultural metamorphosis." The irony is, a metamorphosis is the phase in which a caterpillar turns into a state of mush within the cocoon. To be more scientifically precise, the caterpillar digests itself and, during its transformation, becomes a liquid soup of enzymes. *Merriam-Webster's* dictionary defines the term like this: "the change of physical form, structure, or substance especially by supernatural means." What is happening in our society is not just an attack on the natural identity of children and adolescents but a supernatural attack to break down the identity of man and woman, made in the image of God. It's an attack on God. It is, in fact, the rise of the anti-Christ spirit that will continue to aggressively oppose every facet of our God-given identities and design. This is why it is imperative that in this hour of fierce opposition, we are not only secure in our identity in Christ but armed with the mantles needed for this specific moment in history.

Our culture today is attempting to digest and devour fundamental truths with the ambition to reinvent God's primary design. It is indeed in a state of "metamorphosis," a position the Body of Christ cannot continue to remain silent on. It is, as I write, a supernatural condition of dysphoria and mush. It is no mistake that the terminology *gender dysphoria* is used to describe the current shift away from God's foundational design. Gender dysphoria is described by Webster's dictionary as "a distressed state arising from conflict between a person's gender identity and the sex the person has or was identified as having at birth." The difference between the caterpillar and this state of dysphoria is that God designed the caterpillar to enter the cocoon and emerge a butterfly. He did not, however, design humans to break down the foundations of what He created and attempt to redesign ourselves apart from Him. The result is conflict, distress, and angst.

If you look closely at the origins of these ideologies—not just the push for gender transitioning, but every other issue our society faces today—you will see plainly that they are a direct mockery of the Blood of Jesus. Notice how gender ideologies, for example, promise a rebirth. In fact, that is the exact phrasing I came across when researching "childhood gender transformation" from multiple clinics offering gender-altering surgeries to minors. They promise children a "gender rebirth." It is first and foremost a contemptuous imitation to spit on the Blood of Jesus, to mock those who are born again by His sacrifice. Today, the anti-Christ spirit is alluring an unsuspecting generation with promises to be "born again"—only, aside from Christ, there will be no emerging out of this cocoon as a beautiful butterfly. Rather, they will emerge from this cocoon of goo and find that they are not flying with the wings of free identity that culture sold to them. They will find themselves chained in a worm-like state of depression, anxiety, and crisis.

Without fierce opposition to these destructive ideas, generations years from now will perhaps be the most broken of all generations before them. Our culture is playing with deadly fire, and it's time that the Church fiercely engages in the fight. There is but one answer for this crisis, and His name is Jesus. Only He can transform for His glory that which has been

turned into chaos, and we owe Him all to pursue the generations of today and bring the lost home. By remaining silent, we
do Jesus a disservice, for it is by His Blood that all things are
made right again. Only He can transform that which is broken
and cause this generation to emerge from this cocoon of mush
into the most glorious display of His beauty. This is His plan,
but it will take an army of fierce mothers rising up to say, "Village life may be ceasing, but I will arise as a mother."

How Did We Get Here?

We must understand the spiritual implications and weaponry
being deployed on today's generations through these agendas.
The key word here is *identity*. As stated earlier, if we were to
take a step back and look at every single battle we are facing
and, more importantly, that our children are facing, we would
see it is a war on our God-given identity and a war on God
Himself. As humans made in the image of our Father, the
enemy has cleverly crafted armed forces of words and ideas
to infiltrate the hearts and minds of our generations with the
intent of deconstructing their God-design and reconstructing
his own design. Remember, satan cannot create, he can only
mimic and imitate.

Much like the "safe schools" concept, words have been weaponized in this moment to entice children, especially, with
promises of new existence. This war on identity has leaked
into every facet of life as we know it. We are seeing parents
and teachers alike encouraging this idea of gender fluidity in
their children, some going so far as enticing them into gender

reassignment surgeries. Parents are taking their children along to drag shows in increasing number. Sexually explicit shows that previously only permitted adults to watch are now being embraced by perverted parents, exposing their children to sexualized grooming. We are seeing the term *pedophilia* essentially being reimagined into a more acceptable light, as a "minor-attracted person" (that term is no better in my eyes)—an identity that, we're told, is no different than any other identity and one we should be more accepting of. Not on my watch.

We have seen a growing trend in which the mere mention of the word *woman* makes people uncomfortable, as they are unable to define what a woman truly is. Pregnant women are being erased with the term *pregnant persons*; girls are being pushed out of their own sporting events, replaced with biological males identifying as females. Pornography has been spreading rapidly among our youth, and on applications like TikTok violence and sexual assault against young women have become popular trends and fetishes. Drugs have rapidly invaded these younger generations more than any before them. These same children, raised on the internet and with endless access to entertainment, have all but lost any sense of morality. Violent video games and movies have dulled down their consciences. Young women are embracing a "hook-up culture" as empowerment; then, when she falls pregnant from that one-night stand, she feels further empowered to kill the life of the baby in her womb through what she has been told is her "reproductive right" to murder. In the same notion, there are fewer women desiring to become mothers because society has told them that it's a drawback rather than a gift. We have the horrors of human trafficking increasing globally, and yet we haven't even scratched the surface. Our culture is effectively mutilating our children, whether in the womb, out of the womb, or through the mind. We have allowed a war against their God-given identities, and it has created a worldwide pandemic of its own kind—an insidious deception of dysphoria, confusion, and chaos. What is essential to note here is this spiritual war is not only against the children—it is against the woman. This is why the mantle of Deborah is so important for the hour.

So how did we get here? How did we get to a point in our society where perversion has crept into every facet of life until these conceptions are, like a boa constrictor, squeezing the breath out of our future generations? I believe we as the Church refused to confront these agendas when they were in their seed form. Afraid to offend politically, we have disengaged from a battle we were called to have authority over. Instead of speaking the truth of identity over those who are caught up in these lies, we didn't want to come across as unloving. Through this, we have formed a version of Jesus that is only loving, gentle, and kind. Yet we have refused to acknowledge another important facet of who He is—bold, truth-speaking, unafraid to offend. Jesus was brash in His statements, He was firm on truth, and He never sacrificed love for truth. First Corinthians 13 is often used to justify our retreat in social issues; however, 1 Corinthians 13:6 (NIV) is all too often overlooked: *"Love does not delight in evil but rejoices with the truth."*

I believe there is a holy fire consuming the Body of Christ in this hour, and it is a holiness that will devour every other version of truth, leaving only the infallible truth remaining.

For the love of Christ cannot exist without the truth of God. The Israelites in Deborah's day, as we learned in Chapter One, followed a similar precedent to today's Church. It must have seemed unkind and unloving to them to drive out those the Lord told them to drive out; instead, they dwelt among them. In Judges 4, the first verse says, "*And the people of Israel again did what was evil in the sight of the Lord after Ehud died*" (Judges 4:1 ESV). We too have dwelt among our enemies in the name of being loving and accepting and have participated in evil by overlooking evil. While we are not here to rehearse how bad the world has gotten, I believe it's imperative for us to acknowledge that we have a huge role to play in confronting every demonic agenda that is plaguing society. It's time to take back stolen ground.

They Held Back Until

If you haven't noticed already, I love to investigate the definitions of words and names, both in scripture and in everyday life, for they help me to prophetically see the deeper meanings of what God is saying. I was prompted to look up the name meaning of Mount Lassen, the one I was facing at the beginning of this chapter, the day I was having the conversation with the Lord about the future of my children. To my surprise, I found that Lassen is a German verb that means "to allow, to let, to leave in its current state or condition." The Father was showing me that my role in the future of my children (and this speaks of your role too) was to confront the giants that stood before me, not to allow them to remain in their current state. Like Deborah, you and I must arise and face the giants of our day. Deborah too recognized that village life was ceasing, and it demanded from her a response. She couldn't hide away and ignore it all; she had to arise. We cannot allow these giants to remain in our land; we must also arise and wage war against them. Deborah sang, in Judges 5:7 (NKJV), *"Village life ceased, it ceased in Israel, until I, Deborah, arose, arose a mother in Israel."* The New International Version for this verse transcribes it this way, *"Villagers in Israel would not fight; they held back until I, Deborah, arose, until I arose, a mother in Israel."*

I find the New International Version powerful in this verse. It begs of you the question—who is waiting on your fight? Who is holding back, that you will awaken through your courage to arise? How many other mothers will you influence to step out of their own comfort zones the moment you stand up and fight? Who will follow your lead in standing up and fighting? How many of your children (natural and spiritual) will watch in awe as you arise and, in turn, it will invoke within them a courage to follow? It's time, daughter, to acknowledge that tomorrow fears you. It's time to know you were called to this battle because you were called to claim victory over every mountainous giant that stands in your way. That mountain, that giant, has your name on it because you were called to cast it down. Don't allow it to persist. For the sake of the coming generations, refuse to give it permission to remain in its current state. Stand firm in your position as a daughter of the Most High God, anointed by the Father with this mantle of Deborah, and watch as menacing giants will fall before you. There is an anointing for mothers to arise in this hour and fearlessly stand at the gates of the generations to come and oppose every concept and idea that does not hold to the standard of truth in the Word of God. For if we don't, who will?

Arise, shine, for your light has come, and the glory of the Lord rises upon you (Isaiah 60:1 NIV).

Deborah's Arsenal

Weapon #2: Anointed as a Mother

Deborah did not sit around and wait for someone else to stand up; she recognized her calling. Even though the Bible describes her as a prophet, a judge, and a wife, she does not use any of those terms when she recognizes that the evil of her day required a response from her. She stands up as a mother. God has created within you this same, fierce resolve to stand up and fight like a mother. Just like a mother bear will fight to the death to protect her cubs, God is anointing mothers in this hour to charge upon the enemy's gates without fear or concern for their own welfare, but with a ferocious roar to take back the lost ground of these generations.

The Charge: Acknowledge Where You Are Called

Where do you feel called the most? What issue unnerves you more than any other?

It's important to know what you are called to in this hour; otherwise, you will get overwhelmed by the immense number of issues of our day. Know the ground of culture that God has called you to, and dig your heels in firmly there, trusting that God will show you what to do next.

Once you know the mountain to which you have been called, ask the Lord to tell you what He says over that mountain. Write down His answers. Partner with Him in His solutions. If you ask, He will show you His prophetic word over this mountain, as well as key strategies and solutions in prayer. If you're a mama at home with little ones, your fight might involve prayer and intercession over a particular issue as you go about your day. It may be that He requires you to contact your local school board or representatives. Pay attention to His instructions, because He will always speak His heart intention over the matter, as well as an invitation for you to stand up as a mother and fight with Him in it to see victory over it.

You are called, anointed, and appointed to this hour—you have what it takes. Now, let's get to work!

Note

1. Jenna Wortham, "When Everyone Can Be 'Queer,' Is Anyone?" New York Times, July 12, 2016, https://www.nytimes.com/2016/07/17/magazine/when-everyone-can-be-queer-is-anyone.html.

Chapter Three

I AROSE, A MOTHER

"How will you respond when you are fully, dangerously awake? What history will you make? Will you, like the fierce lioness, awaken from a tranquilized state and rise up to defend your family, your community, your world? Are you awake? Even now, what Is stirring in your heart?"
—LISA BEVERE, *Lioness Arising*

Sunday nights were themed "end times" nights at our church growing up. One of the pastors on staff was the eschatology orator, and every Sunday evening, immediately following worship, he would solemnly approach the pulpit laden with notes about the last days and a prepared power point. Sharing with fiery passion mixed with a heavy sprinkling of fear, he read from varying verses that supported his viewpoint and painted the picture of devastating days to come. I cannot begin to tell you how disturbing this teaching was to my 15-year-old self. Still young in my teenage years, I was beginning to dream of what my life might be like, and at the forefront of those dreams was my desire to one day marry and have children. So you can imagine the effect these fire-and-brimstone messages had on me. I specifically remember one sermon about the mark of the beast and how, as he saw it, it was beginning to be implemented all around the world in, of all places, grocery stores. The pastor then drew our attention to the slideshow he had prepared and began to show us photographs of apparent guillotines that were supposedly being readied in the docks of grocery stores, in preparation for our beheadings there. Grim, I know.

Suffice to say, I went home and cried myself to sleep that night. I vividly remember praying to the Lord, "Of course I want You to return, but please can You let me live a little before You do? I really want to get married and have children. I want a chance to live a life for You." While it's somewhat comedic (perhaps not really) to look back on now, those skewed sermons dimmed my ability to dream with God about the days to come, freezing my heart in fear. What's more, we later discovered that a woman in our church at the time, a mother of three, was so affected by these sermons that she felt called to spend every waking hour—literally, 18 hours a day—locked away in her bedroom preparing for the return of the Lord. While that may sound like a holy assignment, she failed to recognize another important holy assignment right in front of her—her children. She neglected the practical and emotional needs of her own offspring, and they then had to learn to fend for themselves as young as eight years old. We later learned of the situation, and we were told that when she did come out of her bedroom, she did so begrudgingly, which was evidently felt by her children. Today, none of her three children are walking with the Lord because in their eyes God stole their mother from them. Her marriage sadly fell apart, and the last I heard she lives alone without any family around her.

I've often thought of her story throughout the years, because in many ways I feel it reflects the Body of Christ's ill-conceived response to the last days and the assignment right in front of them—a broken world in desperate need of Jesus. I refuse to subscribe to a theology that cloaks us in fear so much that we end up hiding ourselves away while the world goes to hell. Instead, I stand on what Jesus shared in the parable of the talents. In Luke 19:13 (KJV) He said, *"Occupy till I come."* Additionally, through His first miracle of turning water to wine, His wedding-feast sign and wonder pointed to these last days when the wine of the last hours will be greater and richer than the wine of the former.

To quote the author and philosopher Thomas Paine, "If there must be trouble, let it be in my day, that my child may have peace."[1] I feel Thomas' sentiments in this quote entirely reflect my own. I am what you would call an introvert of introverts. I love my space; I don't need a thousand friends or a schedule filled with social gatherings; I don't need my name in lights, and, truth be told, I would prefer to be hidden and unknown. Grateful as I am for influence, it is a never-ending conflict within the natural personality God has given me, which is a preference for anonymity and quiet. However, my preference for peace has been overridden by the calling and mantle of Deborah as it invokes a righteous response within me in this age to which we have been called. I see the threat of the armies on the horizon. Closer they march upon the boundaries of my children and my children's children. Nearer they draw, not laden with swords and spears but with thoughts and contemplations. Perhaps the most insidious army of all time, for a physical army, as daunting as it might be, would be easier to bear, for I could physically see their approach. We could prepare for a physical army with tactical understanding and combat them with machines and weaponry, enlisting armed forces and a country's unified strength. We could hide our children in underground barricades. As terrifying as the situation is, an army of physical force can be seen.

This, however, is a warfare of the mind, one that we need different tools and spiritual weapons for, as well as divine insight, that we might apprehend this military made up of carnal speculations. So if peace must be sacrificed in my time so that my children can one day live in peace, so be it. I'll settle for peace in eternity instead and focus my days on occupying until He comes, for I wholeheartedly believe that the wine of the latter days will be greater than the wine of the former. We are living in days when He is longing to pour out His Spirit as never before.

The Foundation of Deborah's Mantle

Maybe, just like me, you would rather not have to face this enemy onslaught. Who, after all, enjoys warfare? Not anyone

I know. However, unlike the mother who ignored the assignment before her, we can neither ignore what is before us or our role in these last days. If you are alive and reading this book right now, it means that God has chosen you. He specifically hand-selected you for this unique hour. He could have caused you to be born at any time throughout history, but He chose you for now, which means you have been called to this moment and therefore you are being equipped by Him for it. He instilled within you, before you were even born, the qualities you would need for this age. That does not mean you won't feel fear at times, but it means you choose to stand in your calling despite it.

You and I can draw revelation, insight, and courage from Deborah's own bravery as we carry her mantle into the battlefields before us. The words sung by Deborah in Judges 5:7 are a call to you, daughter, a call to responsibility, authority, and action. She sang, "Life in the villages ceased; it ended in Israel until I, Deborah, arose, a mother in Israel." Deborah didn't just see the chaos around her and ignore it or lock herself away. She did not pass the responsibility on to someone else. I imagine she did not desire to go into battle, but the oppression of her people demanded a fierce, motherly response. Deborah recognized the desperate need for godly intervention, so she took up her mantle as a protector, a mother of her people, a defender, and bravely stepped forward. She dedicated herself to occupy the land that had been invaded from enemies within. She couldn't do it alone, though, and we'll learn more about Barak in chapters to come, but there is also another key person she mentioned in the verse just prior, when she sang, "*In the days of Shamgar, son of Anath, in the days of Jael, the highways were abandoned, and travelers kept to the byways"* (Judges 5:6 ESV).

Shamgar son of Anath was also a judge of Israel. His backstory gives us an even deeper understanding of the fierceness of the battle that Deborah waged and, furthermore, the importance of her role in leading Israel back into peace. Merely mentioned in just one verse before Deborah's account in Judges 4, Shamgar is quite an overlooked hero of Judges, and yet the chronicle of his story lays the foundation for Deborah's. In Judges 3:31 (ESV), we read just one telling verse about this judge. It is the very last verse before we cross into Judges 4 that tells of Deborah, so Shamgar's account sets a profound precedent for hers. *"After him was Shamgar the son of Anath, who killed 600 of the Philistines with an oxgoad, and he also saved Israel."*

I would love to read more about him, but the Bible only gives us a mere two verses about this righteous judge. However, they are enough to speak volumes. One could almost say he is the forgotten Samson of Judges, but I digress. His name means "sword," and his father's name, *Anath*, means "answer, song." The ox goad he used to kill 600 men alone is rather an interesting choice of weaponry, but according to Deborah's song in Judges 5:8 (ESV) we find out why—there was no other weaponry available. She sang: *"When new gods were chosen, then war was in the gates. Was shield or spear to be seen among forty thousand in Israel?"* This was a people plundered; they had no defenses left, and it's very easy to understand why. They had chosen new gods and, as such, left the gates wide open for a war within their own territory. Sounds familiar to our day, does it not? Our nations are partnering with horrific mass blood sacrifices through abortion and opening up the gates to gender dysphoria in children, among other abominations. We have invited a war within our own territories.

Our world has chosen new gods; they have chosen new identities aside from God, and they are a people plundered, without protection or spiritual weaponry. Their defenses are down. Deborah's and even Shamgar's battle was, in many ways, much like our own, for the battle they faced was a battle within their own city gates. Without proper weaponry, Shamgar had to find for himself a weapon to fight with. As a side note, it is profound that his name collectively means "a sword, an answer, and a song." He himself became a weapon and an answer that Israel needed and later was mentioned in Deborah's song. Instead of a physical sword, though, he used an ox goad. This was a wooden tool, not necessarily a weapon of their day, approximately eight feet long. At one end, there was a sharp iron spike, which served the purpose of guiding and spurring along the oxen as they pulled the plow for harvest. At the other end, it had an iron scraper to clear lumps of dirt that prevented the plowshare from moving forward. Interestingly, the goad is also referenced in Ecclesiastes 12:11 (ESV), where it says, *"The words of the wise are like goads, and like nails firmly fixed are the collected sayings; they are given by one Shepherd."* And again, in Acts 26:14 (ESV), when Jesus met with Saul on the road to Damascus, it's written, *"And when we had all fallen to the ground, I heard a voice saying to me in the Hebrew language, 'Saul, Saul, why are you persecuting me? It is hard for you to kick against the goads.'"*

First, the verse in Ecclesiastes tells us that the words given by the Shepherd are like a goad. So it's interesting to see the Shepherd, Jesus Himself, mention the goad to Saul. Why did He speak of it here and nowhere else? Saul was a scholar of the scriptures and the law. It would have been a familiar term to him, and therefore he would have immediately understood exactly what Jesus was saying to him. When the oxen would kick against the goad that was guiding them, it was painful and uncomfortable for them to resist because of the sharp iron prod, and Saul was doing just that. He was furiously resisting the prod of the Gospel, and as a result he was experiencing the pain and discomfort of pressing in opposition to the words of the Shepherd. It would have also been a confirmation to Saul that Jesus was the one true Shepherd whose words he had been resisting.

In the same manner, the world of today is resisting the truth of God's Word, and therefore our battle continues to grow fiercer. Second Timothy 3:1-5 (NKJV) gives us a clear account of this resistance of our day:

> *But know this, that in the last days perilous times will come: For men will be lovers of themselves, lovers of money, boasters, proud, blasphemers, disobedient to parents, unthankful, unholy, unloving, unforgiving, slanderers, without self-control, brutal, despisers of good, traitors, headstrong, haughty, lovers of pleasure rather than lovers of God, having a form of godliness but denying its power. And from such people turn away!*

It's any wonder that the world is resisting the message of the Cross in this hour? Their hearts have grown cold as they worship the idol of self. The Word of God is a goad to them because it is the call to surrender, lay down self, and serve the words of the Shepherd alone. It is painful for them as they continue to resist, because try as they may, self can never rule over the one true King. I do believe, however, that in the coming days we are going to see many Saul-to-Paul transformations. Those who have persecuted the Church will be led onto their own roads of Damascus. Damascus means "alertness" and "trade of blood." I believe that as we continue to speak with the goad of His Word, it will awaken those in slumber to a state of alertness, and they will trade in their sins for the Blood of the Lamb. We are truly living in amazing days.

So circling back to Shamgar, these two verses about the goad, together with the account of Shamgar, highlight to us something profound about our foundational role in carrying the mantle of Deborah in this hour. The Word of God is our weaponry in a time when words are being used as weapons against God, His design, and His people. When there is a war on definitions and an attempt to redefine fundamental truths, meanings, and identities, it is the truth of His Word spoken with love that will break the stubborn resistance of the Sauls of our day. Notice that Saul lost his sight on the way to Damascus. In the same way, our world has lost their sight. Jesus is essentially saying to them today, "You are fighting against My Word and My testimony. It's going to be uncomfortable and painful for you to continue to resist." The message of the Gospel is initially agonizing for them to hear, but that does not mean we are to stop sharing the truth. Without it there is no guide, there is no path into the light, and there are only wayward paths that lead the lost to eternal destruction.

Deborah's mantle will carry this foundational weapon of the goad of the Gospel into the fiercest battles of today. Shamgar's battle saw him defeat 600 men. Amazingly, the number 600 in biblical history represents the weapons of war. This key weapon of our warfare is just as Ecclesiastes 12:11 describes it—it is like a nail that firmly hammers the sin of the world to the tree, just as Jesus was nailed in our place. Shamgar's weapon is the foundational bedrock of Deborah's victory, and the Word is the same foundational bedrock upon which we will win the victories of our day. Like the transformative nail that Martin Luther hammered to the door with his "95 Theses," the Word set into motion a cataclysmic reformation. Today, the Word of God will nail down the truth to this generation. It will set into motion a cataclysmic reformation that will redirect a lost and broken world back to the safe and narrow path of truth. His Word is the sword, the goad, the nail, the weapon of our warfare, the answer, and the song that will set the precedent for the mantle of Deborah to drive out the enemies within, making way for the King of Glory. This, daughter, is the very foundation of your assignment in these last days— to know the Word, proclaim the Word, and nail it to every lie. Don't hide it; proclaim it loudly for all to see.

Take Up Your Mantle

Why a mantle? You've probably heard this word thrown around Christian circles and are familiar with it. Particularly in prophetic language, sometimes familiar words can lose the awe and wonder of what they truly mean. A mantle is not just a fun buzz word or a prophetic gimmick that one uses to sound profound. It is, in fact, a very weighty anointing that rests upon a life that is surrendered. When it came to deciding the title of this book, I was honestly conflicted about using the word mantle and wrestled with other words and titles. Throughout the Old Testament, mantles were affiliated with prophets, particularly Elijah and Elisha, and Deborah, too, who was also a prophetess. I wanted to know more, though. With a reverential fear (respect) of the Word of God, I didn't want to just throw around "mantle" for the sake of sounding trendy, and I wanted to know this was legitimately something that the Holy Spirit was speaking into, not just something I was possibly imagining. So I started out on a journey of studying mantles, both in Old and New Testament, to understand how and why this word ties into Deborah and what it means for you and me to carry this cloak. I came across a defining reference written in her account, and this acknowledgement of the mantle happens to be the turning point of battle. It was then that I knew God was confirming the title.

> *And Jael went out to meet Sisera, and said unto him, Turn in, my lord, turn in to me; fear not. And when he had turned in unto her into the tent, she covered him with a mantle* (Judges 4:18 KJV).

This was a significant moment in the battle. It is key to note that this pivotal event happened when the mantle was used.

While we will dig further into Jael's profound narrative later, I want to show you why the mantle is important and how it applies to you as you carry it into the battlefields of today. Let's start at the most notable reference of the word *mantle*, mentioned throughout 1 and 2 Kings with Elijah and Elisha. We're beginning with 1 Kings 19:13 (NIV):

> *When Elijah heard it, he pulled his cloak* [mantle] *over his face and went out and stood at the mouth of the cave. Then a voice said to him, "What are you doing here, Elijah?"*

Now for some context. Elijah had just destroyed the altars of Baal, mercilessly mocked the idols, ruthlessly killed the prophets of Baal, and courageously displayed God's power to a people who had been led astray by a godless queen. This ungodly queen, Jezebel, had raged over the loss of her prophets and set a menacing bounty on Elijah's head. Instead of remaining steadfast in his incredible victory, the mighty prophet ran for his life and ended up hiding in a cave. However, in this cave of intimidation and isolation where he exiled himself in fear, we see a significant mention of the mantle or, as it is mostly translated here, "cloak." I must first highlight what he did with the cloak as soon as he heard the voice of God: *"he pulled the cloak* [mantle] *over his face."*

The word for *cloak* here is the Hebrew word *addereth*, and it means "glory, a cloak, a garment, mantle, a robe." Despite Elijah's cowardice in this instance, God's voice came to him. Remember how we talked about following the voice in Chapter One? In moments of great opposition, there is an invitation

62

to move into greater victories. Yet at these thresholds of victory, you will likely be met with a spirit of intimidation as you move to take the land. I love the way Kris Vallotton says it:

> The dogs of doom stand at the doors of your destiny. When you hear them barking you know you are near your promise land. Most people retreat in fear instead of crossing over and capturing their land. Fear is often disguised as wisdom or stewardship but it is a Trojan Horse sent in to steal your destiny. Fear is not your friend![2]

When I was on that plane on the runway back in Chapter One, I could feel those dogs of doom barking at my destiny. It was the last place I wanted to be. I wanted to stop the plane, run back to the house that we had just packed up, and jump under my bed for comfort and go to sleep. However, as I leaned into His voice, like when Elijah wrapped himself in the glory, His voice, too, covered over my spirit like a cloak of His presence that comforted me. He strengthened me with courage as the plane hurled down the runway. You see, when we are covered by the glory, it is His presence that compels us to come out and go forward. It is His glory that goes before us and prepares the way for us; it is His glory that strengthens us when we feel weak and intimidated by the growling lies of the enemy. We cannot fight these battles without His glory. We will not find victory without Him. We need every ounce of God's glory to consume us, to cover us, and to wrap around us. This is not something we can do on our own. Elijah covered his face in the glory of the mantle because it was his eyes and ears—what he was seeing, perceiving, and listening to—that were in need of truth the most.

Second Kings 1:8 (ESV) gives us a description of what a mantle looked like in ancient Bible times. It says:

> They answered him, "He wore a garment [mantle] of hair, with a belt of leather about his waist." And he said, "It is Elijah the Tishbite."

Pictures of a fur coat come to my mind when I read that description; however, I don't think Elijah's mantle was a fashion statement. I came across this interesting biblical commentary in my studies:

> The servants described the prophet according to his outward appearance, which in a man of character is a reflection of his inner man, as איש בעל שער, vir pilosus, hirsutus. This does not mean a man with a luxuriant growth of hair, but refers to the hairy dress, i.e., the garment made of sheep-skin or goat-skin or coarse camel-hair, which was wrapped round his body...which was worn by the prophets, not as mere ascetics, but as preachers of repentance, the rough garment denoting the severity of the divine judgments upon the effeminate nation, which revelled in luxuriance and worldly lust.[3]

The symbolism of hair gives us further insight into the importance of a mantle. Hair in the Bible typically represents anointing, separation unto God, glory, and strength. It tells us that as we take up this mantle there is a separation that occurs between us and the world. This too, like the goad, is uncomfortable for the world to bear witness to. This garment was rough, not beautiful to behold, and while our King Himself is beautiful to gaze upon, His true and righteous garments are difficult for a world drunk on sin to receive. This does not mean we are to be harsh toward those in darkness, but we are to be harsh on darkness itself.

We see a similar garment made of camel hair worn by John the Baptist. When you consider John's mantle together with Elijah's, the two meld together to paint the picture of our own role as we carry the mantle of Deborah. John was called to prepare the way of the Lord, and you and I, daughter, are called to do the same. There is a cry going out from among God's people in this hour that shouts into the wilderness of society, "Repent, turn aside from your sin, prepare the way of the Lord." Our King is returning; we cannot hide away.

What's amazing about Elijah's story is that, despite his fear of Jezebel, God did not condemn him; He simply asked him, "What are you doing here, Elijah?" Perhaps you are finding yourself in that same cave of intimidation today. The threats are too big, the lies are too enormous, the devastation is too great, the intimidation is too strong, and you've retreated. Whether you've been there for five minutes or for five years, the Lord does not condemn you today. I can hear Him asking, *"What are you doing in that cave, dear daughter? What are you wrapping yourself in, My beloved? Are you wrapping yourself in the convincing lies of fear? Are you covering yourself in stories that have no substance? Are you wrapping your heart and your mind with the threats of the wicked? If so, it's time to come out of that cave. It's time to wrap yourself in the mantle of My glory, cover yourself in My Word, surround yourself with My voice, and lean into My whispers as I lead you and guide you forth. Now, take up your mantle, for I have work for you to do."*

We must put on the cloak of His mantle and make straight His path, call the lost home, and prepare for the coming of our King. We cannot do that when we are hiding in a cave or a room. We can't ignore the roles He has given us. We cannot overlook the high calling of raising our children to do the same. While the world may shout, mock, and taunt us, we must continue to shout all the louder: "Make straight His path." Deborah's mantle is a clearing of the way. She stands in her role as a mother to those around her and points the way to the King. She refuses to allow injustice to remain in her territory, for she sees the high price of the wages of sin—death and eternal damnation. As a mother, she cannot stand idly by and allow her children and her children's children to fall by the wayside; she makes straight the path of the Lord. While sin shouts in opposition and fear screams in trepidation, she continues to move forward, wrapped in the cloak of the Lord.

Are you ready, Deborah? Wrap yourself in the glory of the One who holds you. Wrap yourself in His strong arms and in this mantle to which you have been called.

Deborah's Arsenal

Weapon #3: The Mantle of Courage

Deborah knew that unless she stepped into the position God was calling her to, nothing would change in her nation. She looked and saw that no one was taking charge—they were stuck in apathy. Her song in Judges 5:7 (NIV) said these very words: *"Villagers in Israel would not fight; they held back until I, Deborah, arose, until I arose, a mother in Israel."* Why did the villagers hold back? Fear is often the culprit that keeps us caged when evil is raging. It is courage that calls us to break our agreement with intimidation and be the catalysts of Godly justice and change we are called to be. You will read and discover many things about mantles throughout this book, but one thing I want to highlight is that like Deborah and Elijah discovered, God's mantles carry courage to help us override the fear that would keep us caged.

This is what I feel the Lord saying to you today: *"Take up your mantle even in the face of fear, wrap it around you, and take a bold step of faith in the direction of culture I am leading you into!"*

The Charge: Coming Out of Hiding

What has been causing you to shrink back or *hold back* when you see the battle raging around you? Do you feel unequipped? Has the enemy made you feel small or not up to the task? Do you often feel God has chosen the wrong person and there are many more gifted and anointed people than you?

Write in your journal all the excuses and reasons the enemy keeps speaking to you about why you should stay hidden. What are the main lies he uses to keep you silent and contained? Does this reveal what a threat you are to his plans? How often does he use these intimidation tactics against you in pivotal moments when God is calling you to act and engage?

Next time you hear these lies—when the enemy attempts to lure you back into hiding—remember that your mantle carries the courage of God to get *out* of that confined place. Here are three weapons you can declare over yourself—remembering that you are not depending on your own strength to stand up and fight, but you are depending entirely on God's. He is the One to fill you with courage. He is the One to fill you with the strength you will need to walk in the calling of this mantle:

> *Then he answered and spake unto me, saying, This is the word of the Lord unto Zerubbabel, saying, 'Not by might, nor by power, but by my spirit,' saith the Lord of hosts* (Zechariah 4:6 KJV).

> *But he said to me, "My grace is sufficient for you, for my power is made perfect in weakness." Therefore I will boast all the more gladly about my weaknesses, so that Christ's power may rest on me* (2 Corinthians 12:9 NIV).

> *For I can do everything through Christ, who gives me strength* (Philippians 4:13 NLT).

You are mantled with God's courage, mighty one, so come out of hiding and don't stay there another day!

Notes

1. Thomas Paine, The American Crisis, No. I. https://en.wikisource.org/wiki/The_American_Crisis/The_Crisis_No._I

2. Kris Vallotton, Facebook post, May 10, 2010, https://www.facebook.com/kvministries/posts/pfbid02FnTCJL RYgY2BPG-mrShtxtBt48yz2XAxRNH8K1PCHGqB DW2GnxA3KSnLtXnTtZNhql?__tn__=-R.

3. Carl Friedrich Keil and Franz Delitzsch, *Keil and Delitzsch Biblical Commentary on the Old Testament* (1857-1878), https://biblehub.com/commentaries/2_kings/1-7.htm.

Part Two

THE DEBORAH STRATEGY

Chapter Four

UNDER THE PALM TREE

*Of all things, guard against neglect-
ing God in the secret place of prayer.*
—WILLIAM WILBERFORCE

Recently, I was listening to a friend share on social media how she, her husband, and their children had just moved to "tornado alley" in the Unites States. For those of us in Australia, storms are a normal part of life here. In fact, most of us Aussies love a good summer storm. You see those enormous clouds roll in on a hot afternoon, the breeze begins to cool the day down, and the roar of thunder can be heard echoing in the near distance. I love watching the lightning crack through the sky and the smell of rain as it gets closer; however, tornados are something of a foreign mystery to us. We do get some pretty fierce storms, though, so we often must be prepared for severe hail and flash flooding in low-lying areas. Even so, we tend to just ride out the storms and hope for the best. Australian culture has this mentality of "She'll be right, mate," which in essence is saying, "It will all work out in the end." We prepare, but we are often hit with so many storms that we tend to take it all in our stride. You've probably seen viral videos of Aussies riding what we call "boogie boards," or bodyboards, down flooded storm drains, or men sitting on the roadside with a beer in hand and a sign saying "Splash us" in the hopes cars will swerve into the flooded waters on the roadside and smother them in water.

That said, we aren't foolish either, and when we know a particularly bad storm is on its way or, worse, a hurricane is closing in, we prepare as best we can. However, I don't think we would quite know what to do with a tornado or if our "she'll be right" mentality would work so well in this scenario. Listening to my friend share of how the tornado alarms went off around her home sounded like a bad nightmare. She realized how under-prepared she was with small children and no secure place to hide in their home. Her house at the time had no basement, so she cowered with her children in the bathtub, praying that the tornado would not get close to them. Thankfully, it didn't.

As I listened to her story, I wondered what could be done for protection ahead of time, and out of curiosity I decided to research storm shelters. In my search, I came across a YouTube advertisement for a tornado-proof shelter that can be securely sealed into the foundations of a home, usually fortified in the garage. Even if everything else around the home gets lifted into the raging winds, the storm shelter will remain secure. This shelter looked like a big safe, large enough to fit a small family and a few food and water supplies. In the video, the makers of this storm shelter were displaying all kinds of test scenarios that they were subjecting the shelter to. They were dropping heavy objects onto the shelter—tons of bricks, cars, you name it. They were blasting it with bombs and eruptions, surrounding it with manipulated gale force winds to replicate a tornado, and even firing close range gunshots at it. Despite all the pressures around it, the storm shelter remained unscathed and unmoved, without so much as a scratch affecting the outside of it let alone an ounce of damage to the inside. As I watched in awe, I heard a quiet whisper from the Holy Spirit. He said, "That's what the secret place of My presence looks like. That is where you need to remain in the days to come."

Tornados of Thought

Have you noticed an increase in the swirl of words in recent days? Suddenly everything has a name—everyone has a label, whether good or bad, and these labels have become weapons in and of themselves. You and I are living in days when we are surrounded by dangerous "thought tornados" on every side, and unless we are choosing to spend time in the secret place of God's presence daily, it's going to be very difficult to navigate your way through these storms of manipulated lies. Without the safety of His shelter, you'll find yourself and your family hiding in the bathtub at the last minute, so to speak, probably with a helmet strapped on, waiting, hoping to not get sucked up in the violent winds of rage.

It seems that every way we turn in this unusual hour, there are swirls of tornado-like winds filled with twisted and ungodly ideologies landing upon hearts and minds. Each of these swirls is separately spiraling out of control in chaos and confusion. They are sucking many up with a lure of information, and once they hook you in, you're swept up in their destruction. What may seem like harmless words are in fact spiritual weapons to indoctrinate and destroy God's image-bearers—you and I, His people—and to break down God's design of nations and family. We were made in God's likeness, so it's no wonder that the enemy's number-one tactic is to go after identity from every conceivable angle. We have tornados like anti-choice attempting to vilify those who fight to protect God's image-bearers in unborn babies, tornados of anti-Israel, tornados of race wars, tornados of political wars, tornados of gender confusion, tornados of wars against nations themselves, tornados against freedom, and much more—all swirling across unsuspecting minds, each carrying their own weather systems of thought and speech, each deciphering on their own terms what is right and what is wrong.

Words like *anti-choice* or *religious extremist* are being weaponized to hide these enemy tactics from God's people. These tornados of thought are being manipulated by the enemy to silence us and mask us into submission. Many Christians have become too fearful to speak out on these topics for fear of these tornados descending upon them through the winds of echo chambers—mouths who have been caught up in these lies, who viciously and violently attack those who speak truth. These wind words have been tossed into the sea of humanity like bait, attracting all sorts of vicious sea creatures. One such creature is Leviathan, and another is Jezebel (more about her later, though). These are demonic principalities that are behind all these word wars.

The vicious vitriol of online hate and speech is fueled by the fire of Leviathan's mouth. How do I know this? His fruit is everywhere. Scripture mentions Leviathan several times, and I want to show you the importance of understanding what we are facing so that you will, in turn, discern the importance of being secured in the shelter of the secret place for the sake of you and your family. The world is experiencing a war of fast-moving, destructive, and hyper-speed storms of wind words. If you don't agree with the predetermined narrative of each of these tornados, they will attempt to tear through and destroy every form of morality. These vicious storms of the sea are devouring every unsuspecting ship in their path to magnify their power and repeat their wind words. Take note of how these wind words jump from ship to ship or house to house, repeating the same words again and again. Take abortion, for example. We know that the baby in the womb is a unique, individual human being. However, the wind words of "my body, my choice" have landed upon and sucked into their vortex any common sense. When Leviathan lands, women and men alike in its path repeat and throw around this phrase to justify the inhumane murder of killing their own children. These phrases are the venom of Leviathan.

Without protection, without the shelter of the secret place of the Most High, you are going to find yourself questioning these same thoughts without the understanding of God's wisdom and truth. Sadly, far too many Christians have been sucked up into these thought tornados. The downfall of Roe v. Wade was evidence of that. Not every Christian spends time in the secret place, even leaders. I recently conducted a survey of my Instagram followers and found that out of the thousands who responded, less than 10 percent spend time with God in the secret place daily, even if it's less than ten minutes. That's alarming. This is no time for that Aussie mindset of "she'll be right, mate." We cannot afford to wait for a thought storm to hit us before we rush to find shelter. We must find ourselves in the shelter of His secret place daily. If you are a mother with young children, this may mean you let that basket of washing go unfolded for ten minutes while your baby naps, so that you can open your Bible and rest your soul in His shelter. If you are holding down two jobs, it might mean downloading an audio Bible app and listening to the Word as you commute between jobs or back home again. We must intentionally be seeking God in this hour, or the devourer will seek you out first. Psalm 91:1 must be our mantra for every waking moment of our lives:

> *Those who live in the shelter of the Most High*
> *will find rest in the shadow of the Almighty*
> (Psalm 91:1 NLT).

The Wind Serpent

Leviathan isn't some mystical creature that makes for a good Hollywood blockbuster title. Leviathan is a very real demonic principality that is not to be taken lightly or approached with the Aussie mindset of "she'll be right, mate." Leviathan is explained in a detailed manner in Job 41. I share this not to instill your heart with fear, but so that we might know what we are dealing with and, more importantly, how to combat this enemy principality. No good sergeant major sends his troops into battle without knowing the enemy he is dealing with; likewise, God is giving us wisdom and understanding in this hour to know who we are dealing with and to implement the strategies of heaven to combat this principality.

Job describes Leviathan like this:

> *Can you draw out Leviathan with a fishhook or press down his tongue with a cord? Can you put a rope in his nose or pierce his jaw with a hook? Will he make many pleas to you? Will he speak to you soft words? Will he make a covenant with you to take him for your servant forever? Will you play with him as with a bird, or will you put him on a leash for your girls?* (Job 41:1-5 ESV)

> *Lay your hands on him; remember the battle— you will not do it again! Behold, the hope of a man is false; he is laid low even at the sight of him. No one is so fierce that he dares to stir him up. Who then is he who can stand before me? Who has first given to me, that I should repay him? Whatever is under the whole heaven is mine* (Job 41:8-11 ESV).

> *Who can strip off his outer garment? Who would come near him with a bridle? Who can open the doors of his face? Around his teeth is terror. His*

back is made of rows of shields, shut up closely as with a seal. One is so near to another that no air can come between them. They are joined one to another; they clasp each other and cannot be separated. His sneezings flash forth light, and his eyes are like the eyelids of the dawn. Out of his mouth go flaming torches; sparks of fire leap forth. Out of his nostrils comes forth smoke, as from a boiling pot and burning rushes. His breath kindles coals, and a flame comes forth from his mouth. In his neck abides strength, and terror dances before him. The folds of his flesh stick together, firmly cast on him and immovable. His heart is hard as a stone, hard as the lower millstone. When he raises himself up, the mighty are afraid; at the crashing they are beside themselves. Though the sword reaches him, it does not avail, nor the spear, the dart, or the javelin. He counts iron as straw, and bronze as rotten wood. The arrow cannot make him flee; for him, sling stones are turned to stubble. Clubs are counted as stubble; he laughs at the rattle of javelins. His underparts are like sharp potsherds; he spreads himself like a threshing sledge on the mire. He makes the deep boil like a pot; he makes the sea like a pot of ointment (Job 41:13-31 ESV).

On earth there is not his like, a creature without fear. He sees everything that is high; he is king over all the sons of pride (Job 41:33-34 ESV).

The name *Leviathan* comes from the Hebrew word *Livyatan*, which is derived from a root that means "to twist, to turn, to coil, and also wind." It additionally means, "the joiner" or "to put one and one together" or "logic of thought." Isn't it interesting that it is a creature of the wind, just like those tornados of thought I mentioned earlier? Leviathan uses thoughts and ideologies to twist, turn, and coil against God and all that He is and stands for. Leviathan joins "thought" with a lie, causing logic to twist and coil against the infallible truth. Have you ever seen how a crocodile kills its prey? It clenches down with its mighty jaws upon its unsuspecting victim and then pulls them into a death roll. The death roll is used to dismember its prey as well as to disorient them, making them dizzy so they can't escape. Leviathan has a similar tactic. Through means of the endless news cycles and a barrage of tornados of ideologies and thought, naïve victims are being death rolled into submission to his thoughts and ways, disorienting them from the truth. You will know you have been bitten by Leviathan if you are feeling this sense of "swirling" and disorientation. During the years of 2020 and 2021 especially, his wind words were unleashed as I have never seen them before. The vicious arguing, confusion, and disillusionment was evidence of his poisonous jaws.

Notice that Job's description begins with the weapon of Leviathan's tongue. It is his sword, and he uses it to strike a blow with his ideologies. The chapter then ends with the power of his strength, which is hidden in the high places (idols) through the pride in the hearts of men. Pride is the undergirding of his strength, and you will notice today that pride is often mentioned as a virtue when it is, in fact, the very opposite. Job describes Leviathan like a dragon with a heavy coat of armor that no one can defeat. However, there is only one who can defeat him, and His name is Jesus, and there is hope for you and me as we find ourselves hidden in His shelter. This doesn't mean we are to retreat into a place of fear; it means that our hearts and minds are covered and protected from the barrage of his tornado winds and lies. It means that you will see with clarity what is truth and what is a lie. It means that you will discern with Holy Spirit wisdom how to speak the truth, and you will be protected as you do. However, we have a weapon he cannot conquer, and that is the secret place of God's presence.

Leviathan is mentioned again in Psalm 74, and this verse is very telling of God's strength and power over him. Let's read:

> For God is my King from of old, working salvation in the midst of the earth. You divided the sea by Your strength; You broke the heads of the sea serpents in the waters. You broke the heads of Leviathan in pieces, and gave him as food to the people inhabiting the wilderness (Psalm 74:12-14 NKJV).

While Leviathan is not to be taken lightly, we have this hope hidden in the shelter of His wings—God is the One who will break the head of Leviathan in pieces and give him as food for us in the midst of the battles we face. When the storms of thought tornados come, and they will, make no mistake— you will be prepared. Your family will be secure because you will have your shelter readied under the shadow of His mighty wings. You were not designed by God to be tossed to and fro with the winds of Leviathan; you were called to this moment to reign in the turbulent gales and command them to be still.

Deborah's Secret Place

It is no mistake that we are given Deborah's strategy in the very first verses of her account in Judges 4:4-5 (NIV):

> *Now Deborah, a prophet, the wife of Lappidoth, was leading Israel at that time. She held court under the Palm of Deborah between Ramah and Bethel in the hill country of Ephraim, and the Israelites went up to her to have their disputes decided.*

Deborah was both a prophet and a wife. Even though scripture does not specifically tell us if she was a physical mother of children, given the Hebrew culture of her day that highly valued women as mothers, we can likely assume she was also a physical mother of children as well as a mother to Israel. This description of her speaks of her devotion to God in her calling as a prophet, her role and commitment to her husband and family, and finally her nurturing nature as a mother to the people of Israel. Her husband's name, *Lappidoth*, means "torches and flames." Some have used this meaning to give Deborah the analogy of a "woman of a fiery spirit." I like that description for you and me—"women of fiery spirits." I also see the meaning of her husband's name to describe him as leading with a torch in the dark of night. He is the picture of Jesus here—together, hand in hand, he navigates her through life's darks storms as he holds the torch leading the way. I realize many women reading this book won't have a physical husband by their sides. Perhaps your husband passed or you were left and betrayed by the man you loved and trusted. I want to encourage you here, Jesus is your Lappidoth—He is your torch and flame. As you cleave yourself to Him, He is the one who will guide you on the right paths with the flame of His Spirit.

What I love about Deborah is she is divinely balanced. What I mean by that is, she carried each of her roles with grace. Our world today tells a woman that to be successful she has to murder her children, begrudge men, and do whatever she can to get to the top. In a recent documentary on Marilyn Monroe, it was shared how she stood in the crowds of adoring fans and, with tears streaming down her face, whispered to herself, "For this, you killed your children." Feminism has been one of those destructive tornadoes of ideology that has convinced women to destroy the very gift God gave them as bearers of life and murder their own infants. I understand that there are women reading this book who have gone through with an abortion or even multiple abortions. I want you to hear my words loud and clear. I am not casting shame upon you when I speak of these things. I am merely bringing light to the hidden darkness that has been unspoken for far too long—and where there is light, there is freedom to be found. I pray you would hear the words of Jesus over you right now: "Daughter, your sins are forgiven. Go and sin no more." The enemy has snared a generation of women into the lie of abortion—that it is their right to murder their own young. Then, when they have followed through with that lie, he has cast them down into shame, guilt, and condemnation. No more, daughter, are you to wear these clothes of condemnation, for Jesus is robing you with this mantle of Deborah. It is a mantle of restoration, vindication, and justice. You will slay these principalities by His Blood and by the Word of your testimony. Your baby prays for you in heaven as a part of the great cloud of witnesses. I see you speaking to the tornado words of feminism that have shackled other women, and I see you breaking them free by your testimony. It's time to step into your freedom.

Feminism has left a wake of destruction, much like the path of a tornado, over a generation of women, reducing them into murderers of their own children, angry, vile-hat wearing, men-despising echo chambers of vicious thought and speech. This is not who you are. You are called to be a daughter of the Most High, echoing His truth, applied with His love. Whatever your story, God is anointing you, daughter, with the mantle of Deborah in this hour and positioning you with strategy for the days ahead. Deborah wore the mantle of her two roles with grace, which is what God is calling you to. A daughter who is hidden in the secret place of His heart, a daughter who is given grace by Him to hold the multiple roles He has called you to, you will carry them with His ease. It may not always be easy, but there will always be sufficient grace to glean from Him.

Weighing Thoughts and Intentions from the Secret Place

I want you to pay specific attention to Deborah's position here, for it gives us this key strategy for our role in carrying this mantle. The two verses of Judges 4:4-5 immediately poise Deborah with the strength of her roles and the strategy of her position. Allow me to show you how. Let's read Judges 4:5 (NIV) again for context:

> *She held court under the Palm of Deborah between Ramah and Bethel in the hill country of Ephraim, and the Israelites went up to her to have their disputes decided.*

Let's first look at the Hebrew words used for "held court," which is also translated to say "she would sit" under the palm. It is the Hebrew word *yashab* (Strong's H3427)—this word means, literally, "to dwell, abide and convene, to inhabit and sit in peace; to be married to, to remain, to be a resident of." Do you see how this links in with the strategy of the secret place? What is the secret place then? It is the habitation of God's dwelling; it is where He invites you and me to convene with Him, talk with Him, and make room for Him in our days.

I mentioned earlier that you need to find those small daily increments of time to read your Bible, but I also want to highlight to you that the secret place is the place you *remain* throughout your day. Don't leave there. You may not be physically lying on the floor in His presence all day long, but your position is one that continues to convene with Him throughout the day. When you are working or tending to your children or cooking dinner or studying at college, your mind is fixed and stayed on Him. "How do I do that?" you might ask me. Through repetition. When you wake up in the morning, before opening your phone or checking the news, turn your heart toward Him.

With saying that, be careful of what your eyes are looking at throughout the day. Are you watching horror movies? Because that is an easy way to unseat you from that position of peace. Are you reading the newsfeeds on your social media all day long? Again, you'll find yourself in that windswept place of fear rather than by the calming streams of His presence. The definition of *abide* means to "continue for a long time, to endure." It is the practice of being in His presence that keeps you protected from the onslaught of lies that will surround you in culture. It is this habitual choice to keep in constant communion with your Creator, God, that will enable you, like Deborah, to discern with truth the disputes that you see swirling all around you.

This was Deborah's first and most important strategy—to dwell in the presence of God—and it is this very position that poised her for victory. I'll address the significance of the palm tree in just a moment, but first I want to highlight the meanings of Ramah, Bethel, and Ephraim. Notice that Deborah was "dwelling" under the palm tree between Ramah and Bethel. *Ramah* means "high and exalted." This may be somewhat of a rabbit trail here, but I want you to consider with me something important that was mentioned about Leviathan. Do you remember in Job 41:31 how it told of Leviathan's position, his strategy? It tells us that "he sees everything that is high" and he is "king over all the sons of pride." This is an interesting parallel here, because we find Deborah sitting between a place called *Ramah*, meaning "high and exalted" or "lofty place," and Bethel. This tells me that she was weighing the high and exalted places when she held court. Now Bethel, on the other hand, means "house of God." Deborah was weighing and balancing disputes, much like a scales of justice, and discerning between what was a high and lofty lie on one side and what was truth according to the house of God on the other. Had she not been positioned in peace in the secret place under the palm tree, she would not have been able to discern what was right, what was true, and what was deserving of Godly justice.

Deborah was also positioned in the hill country of Ephraim, which means "to be fruitful." Again, looping back to an earlier mention in Chapter One, you may remember how God assigned the tribe of Ephraim to cast out the enemy inhabitants and they failed to do so, rejecting the prophetic promise upon their life "to be fruitful." Deborah however, was positioned in the hill country of fruitfulness as a divine messenger of recompense for what was lost in previous years. This is important to take note of. It paints a beautiful picture of the fulfillment of God's promises despite the failure of others. The Lord always will find a way to see that which He has promised brought into fulfilment.

Perhaps you have failed to follow His calling in years gone by, and you are wondering, *Will I ever see that promise fulfilled despite my failure?* The answer is yes. As you surrender to the secret place, God is positioning you in the hill country of "fruitfulness" to see the promise fulfilled.

The Doors to the Secret Place

Finally, I want you to see the importance of the palm tree in Deborah's story. Some might assume Deborah just sat herself under some pretty tree for the sake of shade, but that is far from the picture being painted here. Everything in scripture has incredible prophetic insight and symbolism, and the palm tree is no different. I want to take you on a brief journey through scripture to understand the powerful strategy hidden for us here. In 1 Kings 6:29-32 (NIV) we are told:

> *On the walls all around the temple, in both the inner and outer rooms, he carved cherubim, palm trees and open flowers. ...For the entrance to the inner sanctuary he made doors out of olive wood that were one fifth of the width of the sanctuary. And on the two olive-wood doors he carved cherubim, palm trees and open flowers, and overlaid the cherubim and palm trees with hammered gold.*

The palm tree is a prophetic allegory of the doors to the inner sanctuary and the walls that lined the temple. As we now know, under the covenant of the New Testament through Jesus' Blood you and I have become the living temples of the Holy Spirit. Lining the walls of our temples are the cherubim, a picture of angelic protection; the palm trees, a picture of salvation; and the open flowers, speaking of a sweet fragrance and fruitfulness in Christ. The doors to the inner sanctuary were also lined with all three of these pictures, which again speaks of the doors to your heart, covered and protected by angels, and your salvation found in Christ Jesus. It is the entrance of your inner sanctuary, your secret place of communion with God.

The fact that Deborah sat under the palm tree in between the high and lofty places and the house of God tells us that her salvation, her communion with God in the secret place, was a guard against the evil that she sat in the middle of. Daughter, you don't need to fear the darkness that surrounds you—the darkness fears you.

Deborah's Arsenal

Weapon #4: The Secret Place

The call of Deborah wasn't one of brash, sporadic, or reactionary responses to the issues she faced in the world but one of security, peace, and confidence in God. Her secret weapon—that her enemy does not have—is the presence of the Most High. When she dwelled under the wings of the Almighty it turned the tide of the battle because she was no longer fighting from her own strength or abilities but rather resting entirely in her Father's. This will always be Deborah's greatest weapon because it's her surrender to God that enables His power to flood into her like a conduit. Her ability to rest in the secret place with God empowers her to overcome every adversity that she faces.

The Charge: Live from His Presence

Are you living from the secret place or from your own strength? Do you often burn out quickly when facing warfare or an obstacle in your life? Do you get flustered, anxious, and make bad decisions when the battle rages, or do you lean into His presence?

Write in your journal a list of the fruit you have seen in your life when you don't live from the secret place. What is the cost you pay for not investing time to be filled with His presence and His Word? Has there been a time recently when you realized that you needed to be living from the overflow of His presence, but instead you were running on empty?

Write down a few examples of what happens when you are living in His presence in the secret place. How does it change the battle?

Next time you face an impossible situation or encounter demonic opposition, don't react right away; take a step back, and lean into the Lord. Imagine yourself like Deborah under the palm tree of His presence, then wait for His instruction and it will surely come.

Chapter Five

THE OFFENSIVE BATTLE PLAN

"God wishes for us a heroic faith, a faith that requires not only prayers but actions, too, just as any child or any fool already knows, but which some perversely religious persons have not known, tragically confusing millions."
—ERIC METAXAS, *Bonhoeffer: Pastor, Martyr, Prophet, Spy*

Nate and I and our girls were in Sydney, Australia, this past week, and while we were there an Australian rugby Grand Final Premiership was taking place just a few suburbs away from where we were staying. The streets were filled with crowds wearing their team colors, and people were shouting and reveling in excitement as the game drew closer. It feels kind of strange to be writing about sports as I'm not the committed type of a sporting fan. I've been to a handful of games in my life—a Dallas Stars ice hockey game, an LA Lakers basketball game, and an Anaheim Angels baseball game, and that is it. All merely for the novelty of it. I enjoyed the electric atmosphere but never walked away with the sporting bug, so to speak. Australians are die-hard sporting fans, so it's almost offensive to my countrymen to have never even been to an Aussie game, but it is what it is. I did play a lot of sports in school, but faithfully following a team has just never been something that has been on my radar. It is extremely rare for me to watch a game on television too. However, being in the electric atmosphere in Sydney during this premiership, I was intrigued by it all, so I turned on the television when we got back to our hotel room to find out more about it. I came to discover this wasn't just a normal Grand Final either. One of the teams that was in the lineup, known as the Parramatta Eels, hadn't been in a Grand Final since 2001, which they had lost. No wonder the atmosphere was so charged. This was a huge deal for the Eels fans. They had faithfully followed their team through loss and disappointment for years, and now they were poised to finally, hopefully, claim a victory.

After putting our littlest daughter to bed, Nate and I tuned in to watch the game later that night. My natural inclination was to cheer for the Eels as the underdog. As little as my affections are for any sporting game, I was hoping to see a victory for them. We had missed the first half of the final while putting Ava to bed, so we tuned in quite late, and my heart sank when I saw the scoreboard (not a lot, I'll add, but a little out of empathy). The opposing team was already light years ahead, having scored around 21 tries (if a "try" is even what it's called—I'm sure someone reading this is annoyed at my incorrect phrasing), with the Eels not even making a single try yet. Even as inexperienced with sporting games as I am, I knew that it was difficult for the Eels to win at this point. Nate and I watched the remainder of the game as the Eels desperately tried to hold on to the ball and make a try, or a touchdown, or whatever it is called. Each time they made it to the end of the field, though, they were tackled ruthlessly by the opposing team and they would lose the ball, securing only a few tries. You could see the defeat and desperation in their eyes, as they all knew the game was all but lost.

The one thing that stood out to me was the fact that they continued to lose the ball, it was almost as though the ball was covered in slippery butter and they just couldn't seem to hold on to it. In fact, one of the main news headlines about their ultimate defeat read, "They dropped the ball." In reading this article, something else stood out to me. Sports commentators remarked that the team made two odd decisions in the lead-up to the game. The opposing team made time to train in the stadium where the Grand Final was to be held; the Eels, however, did not. They chose to continue their training in their regular training grounds of comfort and familiarity. The other point that was mentioned was that on the day of the final, the team did not bus together into the Grand Final stadium; instead, they each took their own separate cars to make their way there, driving in alone. The sports commentator added, "That's where they first dropped the ball—they treated this game like any other game." It wasn't even in the stadium where they lost the game—it was in the preparation.

Now, I recognize we are not playing in a game; the battle we are engaged in is serious spiritual warfare as opposed to rambunctious play. However, the lessons that can be drawn from their defeat remind me of something I shared about in my first book, *Releasing Prophetic Solutions*. In my late 20s, desperate for direction about my flailing and struggling spiritual and prayer life, I happened to stumble across a book by Beni Johnson called *The Happy Intercessor*. I remember that title standing out to me because I knew I was called to prayer, but I was miserable in it. I didn't enjoy prayer at all; I found myself weighed down with the worries and cares of the world, and I avoided conversations with God as a result. I wasn't prepared for the battles I was engaged in. You could say I was a lot like the Eels in my prayer life—prayer was like that slippery ball that I was desperately trying to keep a hold of but kept failing to score any victories with. I felt all but defeated. The words *happy* and *intercessor* put together sounded more like an oxymoron, but that book would become one of the more defining books of my life, aside from the Bible, of course.

Before we highlight the importance of Beni's point, I want to take a moment to honor the wonderful life of Beni Johnson and the mark she left on my own life. Though I knew her personally only briefly, the impact of her full life of prayer was cataclysmic upon my own. Her teachings on prayer and intercession were like that of Deborah to me. She charged where no one else was, paved new territory, sat under the palm tree in the secret place with the Lord, and as a result boldly led a generation of both men and women to take down the giants in their own lands. I am so thankful for her words that continue to echo into eternity. I'm not sure I would even be writing this book if it were not for the paths she bravely forged that lit up the way for others, like me, to walk upon. I have no doubt her mission in prayer continues from the heavenly advantage she is now sitting in. So from the bottom of my heart, thank you, Beni. Thank you for your life laid down in love to Jesus and your time with Him in the secret place. Your fruit continues to blossom in the lives of others, mine included, like a ripple effect. I am forever grateful.

I shared this paragraph in the first chapter of my first book, and I feel this point is poignant enough to make mention of again. Beni wrote in her book:

> On a football team there is a defensive team and an offensive team. The defensive team tries to steal the football from the opposing offensive team. The defensive team will try to figure out the offensive team's strategies and plays. The offensive team, however, has the advantage in that they have the ball. With their skill and different plays, they proceed to carry the football down the field to make a touchdown. The offensive team calls the plays, for they have the ball. ...For intercessors, it is extremely important to understand that God has already given us the ball. We are the offensive team. If you don't understand that, if you are not

praying from a place of victory, then you will be an intercessor whose prayer life is marked with defeat. You will be one who is always trying to protect what God has given you from the devil's plans, or worse yet, running after the devil and trying to figure out what he is doing. How wrong is that? If you do not understand that God has already given you the ball, you will live in fear and pray from a place of lack.[1]

Beni's description about the offensive prayer life was transformative for me. It completely flipped the narrative on how I had been praying. While I know Australian rugby and American football have different rules, the principles remain the same. The Eels had gone into their Grand Final and, as the commentator said, dropped the ball of their victory before they even got onto the field. The Eels "treated this game like any other game." That one remark holds a key for us in the battles we are facing with this generation. The Eels failed to recognize the unique strength of their opponents. Could they have defeated them? Absolutely, with the right strategy. However, they depended upon old strategies, and it was made immediately evident in the first quarter just how much of a crucial mistake that was.

These battles we are in are unlike any other behind us. While I have no intention of keeping the focus on our enemy, we must not underestimate what we are dealing with. Peter instructs us in 1 Peter 5:8 (NIV), *"Be alert and of sober mind. Your enemy the devil prowls around like a roaring lion looking for someone to devour."*

The Greek words that Peter used in these verses highlight to us the importance of being clear-minded about who we are dealing with. *Sober-minded* is the Greek word *nepho* and it means "to be free from illusion, to have clear judgment, to not be intoxicated by the illusions of the world" (Strong's G3525). The Greek word Peter used for *alert* is *grégoreó* and it means "to be awake in the night, to be watchful, on the alert, and vigilant" (Strong's G1127). I wonder, did the Eels go into their game with illusions? Did they assume they had the game in the bag? Did they rest upon their past victory that won them their place in the Grand Final?

While we rest upon the strength of the One who has *all* authority, we must remain vigilant in our prayer life and free from the intoxications of this world. We cannot go into this with a sense of pride that "we have the battle in the bag." We must come at this from a unique standpoint—a humble reverence for God and a position of surrender to Him. Otherwise, we too will find the ball of our authority slipping from our hands. We cannot depend on past victories to get us over the finish line here; we need unique and divine strategy from God for the days ahead. We cannot lean on old revelation from yesterday. Just as the Israelites had to pick up fresh manna daily, we too must eat of the fresh manna of His Word every single day. We need divine revelation, and that will only come from being in the secret place with Him. We cannot stay in old places of comfort; we must move into new territory. Sometimes that will mean following Him into new, occasionally uncomfortable terrain.

Finally, an imperative strategy in the battles we face today is that we need each other—we cannot travel into these battles alone. If we do, we will find the generations of tomorrow slipping between our hands. We need the strength of the army, we need each other, and as we will find in this next section Deborah too understood this principle.

Offensive Strategies

How do we move in offensive strategies in our day? Let's look at how Deborah strategized with God. Deborah recognized that she needed divine strategy for the battle at hand. Here is what she said to Barak, the commander of Israel's army, in Judges 4:6 (ESV):

> *She sent and summoned Barak the son of Abinoam from Kedesh-naphtali and said to him, "Has not the Lord, the God of Israel, commanded you, 'Go, gather your men at Mount Tabor, taking 10,000 from the people of Naphtali and the people of Zebulun.'"*

We're going to camp around this verse for a moment. While it may not appear at face value to contain any kind of strategy, it does indeed reveal insight into the divine scheme that the Lord gave Deborah. We're going to break down this verse strategy by strategy.

1. *Deborah didn't march alone.*

She sent and summoned Barak the son of Abinoam from Kedesh-naphtali.

Barak's name means "lightning and thunderbolt." When you think of lightning, what comes to mind? Awe, fear, wonder? I have always loved watching storms from a distance. You can see the vast enormity of the storm as it rises into the sky, and the lightning dances within the clouds in a display of God's glory. Up close, however, lightning is a lot more fearsome, especially when a storm is directly overhead. I've seen lightning bolts strike within ten feet away, and I've watched an entire fence explode from just one strike. The mere sound of a strike is deafening, so it's very fitting that Barak's name means "lightning and thunderbolt." In scripture, lightning is representative of God's presence. It also speaks of His wrath against His enemies and the strength of His power.

Psalm 144 provides a descriptive vision of the effect God's lightning has on an enemy army. In verse 6 (ESV) it says, *"Flash forth the lightning and scatter them; send out your arrows and rout them!"* Interestingly, Deborah and Barak coming together in this divine alliance paints for us the picture of an incoming storm for the enemies of God, in which His lightning will cause them to scatter in a million directions.

For you, I believe the Lord is highlighting the importance of divine alliance with others who are called to this battle. Coming together, unifying in prayer and action under the banner of Jesus to scatter the demonic forces that are at work within our generations. Notice how today's modern feminist movement seeks to destroy men. I find it compelling that Deborah called upon a man to move into battle, and he in return called upon her to fight alongside him. God's antidote for the destructive ideologies that modern feminism has produced is, not so ironically, men and women coming together, fighting alongside one another, and declaring as one for the Kingdom of God to be established.

It's also interesting that Deborah's name means "a bee." The bee prophetically speaks as one singular bee in an army of bees. It's why the Lord is releasing Deborah's mantle over His daughters in this hour—because He is not seeking to rest this anointing upon just one daughter but many. The strength of a beehive is found in the unified force of each individual bee. Together, they work to extract the pollen (the Word of God), they direct one another to new sources of nectar (they share in the strategies the Lord gives them), they build together (they build up their communities), and they protect their young together (they raise families in the Kingdom together and fight off invaders who attempt to rob the hive). As one, they follow their queen if she leads them to swarm. In our case, we follow our King, and our strength is in our numbers.

There is a swarming taking place right now as the Lord is calling you out of isolated separation, where you have stood alone. He is calling you to follow Him into the unknown, follow the sound of the swarming. In other words, follow where you see others leading, and then be a voice in return—call out to others behind you, call them to join you. This is a season of time when we won't see just one voice on the pulpit leading the multitudes into spiritual battle, but there will be many voices leading the charge. That's you, daughter. You have a voice, and God is calling you to use it. Your voice matters. This is a season of unification. It is the oneness of His Bride that will attract the very presence of God, and like Barak's lightning He will strike the enemy from within our midst, scattering and routing demon forces wherever we tread.

Before we dive into the significance of the next point, we need to take a quick look at where Barak came from, "Kedesh-Naphtali," because this location, just like the significance of Deborah's location, gives keen insight into knowing whom to align with. Not everyone will be for you, and not everyone is called to this specific mantle, but you can take some insights from Barak when discerning whom God is calling you into battle alongside. *Kedesh* means "consecrated, set apart, to be holy, sacred place." You will know whom to align with because they will live an offensive lifestyle of consecration. Look for those who are living in this offensive manner, whose very foundations are built upon the sacred place of God's presence—those who spend time with Him and whose lives reflect His holiness.

In contrast, *Naphtali* means "my wrestling" and "crafty one." There is a wrestling that we must engage with together. It's not promised to us that this wrestling will be easy, but we are promised that God will be with us in this wrestling, and He will give us crafty and cunning solutions for the hour at hand. Search for those who are willing to look offensive to the world, seek out those who have consecrated themselves to the Holy One, and with them you will find that God releases His prophetic solutions to you as you move in unison together.

2. Deborah discerned the terrain.

*Has not the Lord, the God of Israel, commanded
you, "Go, gather your men at Mount Tabor."*

Mount Tabor was a strategic location in ancient biblical times. It was stationed in the middle of extremely rich and fertile land known as Jezreel. Today, it remains a lush and fruitful ground that is vastly used for farming. Mount Tabor rises out of the midst of the Jezreel Valley like a huge dome that cannot be missed. It is seen from all territories in the region, jutting out of endless flat plains like a huge sore thumb, rising a little less than 2,000 feet above sea level. Jesus Himself was familiar with Mount Tabor. He and the disciples would have traveled around this mountain many a time in their journeys. In fact, numerous biblical scholars believe that because of its location and proximity to other key locations in the New Testament, it was on this mountain that the transfiguration of Jesus occurred. This would make sense given the meaning of Tabor's name, which is "to purify and to clarify." If it was indeed upon this mountain that the transfiguration took place, it tells the story of the fullness of His identity coming into full clarity before the three disciples who were with Him on the mountain that day. It also speaks of His destiny on the Cross, where His Blood would purify the sins of the world.

So given these insights, how does Mount Tabor hold a strategy for Deborah and, in turn, for us today? Mount Tabor sits in the middle of the Jezreel Valley. It's worth digging a little bit deeper into the meaning of Jezreel's name as well. I know what you may be thinking: "Really, Christy? Another meaning and definition?" Why, yes. If you've gotten to know me even a little by now, you will know how I love to dig into the Word and not just look at it at face value. These names, their locations, and their meanings are not there by chance. Everything God writes is incredibly poetic and like a tapestry is linked to deeper insights and wisdom.

Therefore, in the story of Deborah, Jezreel and Mount Tabor are no different. *Jezreel* means "the God who sows." It comes from the verb *zara*, which means "to scatter seed," and from the word *el*, which is a name of God. The verb *zara* can also mean "offspring, posterity, family, and community." I find it amazing that Deborah discerned what was at stake: the legacy of Israel—children, families, communities. She recognized the severity of the battle at hand and understood their immense need for God's intervention. *Zara* can additionally mean "he who scatters the chaff and debris."

Deborah led the battle to the valley of the God who sows, knowing that only He could save their future. She led the battle to Him who scatters the chaff and debris, knowing that only He could scatter their enemies. Was it any coincidence that she chose this location? A place that represented the seeds of children, family, and legacy, and additionally a position that is overshadowed by God—He who sows the seeds and He who scatters the chaff? This was no coincidence—this was offensive strategy.

In addition to Jezreel, she strategically rallied the troops on the top of Mount Tabor, a place that represents purification and clarification. They needed to be purified in His presence, and they needed clarity for the war they were about to wage.

Deborah didn't spin a globe and randomly throw her finger on the map in the hope of finding a good place to rally the troops; this was intentional. Because of her position in the secret place with God under the palm tree, she was acutely in tune with the voice of God, and it was He who directed her to assemble their army atop this mountain in the middle of this specific valley. This was God's offensive battle plan.

Have You Dropped Your Ball of Authority?

There is a strategic, key question in Judges 4:6, which Deborah points to Barak. Let us look at the verse as a whole one last time before we move into the next chapter.

> *She sent and summoned Barak the son of Abinoam from Kedesh-naphtali and said to him, "Has not the Lord, the God of Israel, commanded you, 'Go, gather your men at Mount Tabor, taking 10,000 from the people of Naphtali and the people of Zebulun'"* (Judges 4:6 ESV).

Did you see it? *"Has not the Lord, the God of Israel commanded you?"* Barak, like our Australian rugby team, had dropped the ball of God's promise of victory before he even got onto the field. Was it out of fear? Most likely. Yet despite his wavering fears, God strengthened him by bringing Deborah alongside of him. The Lord had already given him this command, and like the slippery hands of the Eels, he had dropped it. I wonder, though, how long had Barak been sitting on this command? It could have been days, months, or even years.

Regardless, it reveals the faithfulness of God to complete what He started and bring deliverance to His people despite any irrational fears that may freeze us for a moment.

I want to pose this same question to you today—have you dropped your ball? Has not the Lord already commanded you? Have you dropped your authority? Have you been sitting on a prophetic word and not known what to do with it? Or have you been frozen in fear? I believe there is an anointing that comes with this mantle of Deborah to break you out of any irrational (or even rational) fear and raise you up in courage again. I hear the Holy Spirit reminding you today, "Pick it up again, daughter. Pick up what I have given you. I am faithful to finish what was started in you, but you must pick it up."

Once you do pick up what He has commanded you, how do you engage in this battle? How can you discern the terrain we are in? Unlike Deborah, ours is not a battle in which we can physically lead our enemies to a physical war of drawn swords, arrows, and spears, for the warfare we are facing today is largely spiritual. How then do we fight a spiritual battle in a natural world? We find the answer to this question in 2 Corinthians 10:4-6 (ESV). These verses hold for us our offensive battle plan:

> *For the weapons of our warfare are not carnal but mighty in God for pulling down strongholds, casting down arguments and every high thing that exalts itself against the knowledge of God, bringing every thought into captivity to the*

obedience of Christ, and being ready to punish
all disobedience when your obedience is fulfilled.

I'll be revisiting and divulging the practical strategies of this verse in coming chapters. For now, I must stress this point—you must be prepared for both prayer and action. This battle *will* require both. Not the kind of action where you are drawing a sword against those who oppose you, but the kind where you are engaging in the public sphere, using the Word of God as the weapon of your warfare. The public sphere has been ignored by the larger Church for too long. We have chosen, like the Israelites, to live among our enemies (speaking of demonic ideologies here). It's time we ask the Lord for forgiveness for permitting idolatry where it doesn't belong, and drive out these demon forces from our midst. Ours must be a strategic, offensive battle plan. We must be positioned in Jezreel and on Mount Tabor in spirit. Our hearts must be consecrated and set apart for purification so we can see with clarity the spiritual layout of the battle. You might ask, "How do we do that?" You're going to have to practice being in the secret place with God. It all comes back to this foundation, for without the strength of this foundation you will find you have no footing when He leads you to the heights of the mountains to wage war.

It was in the secret place, just as Deborah discovered, where strategy was revealed. Isaiah 30:21 (NIV) says, *"Whether you turn to the right or to the left, your ears will hear a voice behind you, saying, 'This is the way; walk in it.'"* Deborah heard the voice. She listened and followed accordingly. Notice that the voice comes from behind. It's because you are meant to walk forward and not sit still in stagnation. Ezekiel tells us in Ezekiel 43:2 (NIV), *"and I saw the glory of the God of Israel coming from the east. His voice was like the roar of rushing waters, and the land was radiant with his glory."* His voice is ever moving, ever rushing like a river, and unless you are in that river you will not be flowing with the movement of where He is leading you for this specific moment in history. Get in the river, daughter—don't wait, jump right in. Run into the secret place of His presence, under the palm tree of His strength. Position yourself in Him, for the hour is at hand when He is calling you to take back the land.

Deborah's Arsenal

Weapon #5: Prophetic Strategy

Deborah wasn't acting randomly in her approach to battle, nor was she unplanned or improvising as she went—she was wisely making decisions according to the instruction of the Lord that always kept her a few steps ahead of her enemy. She did this by living in the presence of God (under the palm tree, the secret place), and from there she received the prophetic strategy, intel, and insight to know how to defeat her intimidating foes. Your battle plan can only come from this posture and from that position. The Holy Spirit will come alongside you and whisper to you the divine strategies needed to take down the enemies around you.

The Charge: Live Offensively

Do you often feel like you are never ahead of the enemy but find yourself caught by surprise and bewildered in the aftermath of his attacks? Do you get frustrated that you rarely discern his tactics and have become used to being taken down regularly?

Here's something to help you. First, decide that you are no longer going to be the victim in the situation or the helpless person in the equation—reject that role. Now ask the Lord to give you a new stance in the spirit. Ask the Holy Spirit to show you areas where you have been taking matters into your own hands and living reactionary, rather than living in a pre-emptive lifestyle of prayer. He will show you practical ways to stop being blindsided and robbed over and over again, and show you how to see with eyes of the spirit that see the enemy afar off and give you strategies to catch him out.

Note

1. Beni Johnson, *The Happy Intercessor* (Shippensburg, PA: Destiny Image Publishers, 2009), 39-40.

Chapter Six

THE HIGH PLACES

"Some Christians are afraid to discuss spiritual warfare because they believe it makes evil forces stronger. The truth is that our enemy is already operating at full strength, and by exposing his deeds of darkness, we diminish his power, not increase it."
—LISA BEVERE

Reading through the Old Testament can sometimes be a little daunting. Words, phrases, names, and places can often sound incongruent and not relatable to our modern lives today. For that reason, it can be easy to neglect the important messages and warnings throughout Old Testament stories as they pertain to us in this present age. One such warning is found repeatedly in what was known as "high places." High places were mentioned often, and yet I rarely hear them preached about in sermons today. When you see a high place in scripture, it was not in reference to a pretty outlook that an influencer you follow on social media has climbed to take a good Instagram photo from. It was in association with a place of worship and spiritual authority. High places were primarily used as physical locations of worship dedicated specifically to idol worship. They were positioned on high mountains or hills where people would sacrifice to their gods as a declaration for all to see. These sacrifices often included their very own firstborn babies thrown into fire. These high places usually consisted of shrines, altars,and incense burning and were places dedicated to graven images. However, the location was not always a mountaintop; sometimes these high places were built at city gates or common places where many people passed by. By creating these high places in mass traffic areas, it normalized idol worship for many of God's people.

If you're wondering about the origins of a high place, look no further than Isaiah 14:12-13 (NIV), where the Lord is speaking to lucifer (whom we now call satan). In these verses, God plainly highlights the very reason for lucifer's fall:

> *How you have fallen from heaven, morning star, son of the dawn! You have been cast down to the earth, you who once laid low the nations! You said in your heart, "I will ascend to the heavens; I will raise my throne above the stars of God; I will sit enthroned on the mount of assembly, on the utmost heights of Mount Zaphon."*

Today, satan, continues to think like this; he continues to attempt (and fail) to raise himself above God. Notice he said he would sit on the "utmost heights" of a mountain. In his stupidity, he thought he could raise himself above the one true God by merely sitting himself on top of a mountain. Pretty dumb logic when you think about it. Interestingly though, he chose Mount Zaphon as the place of worship to himself. *Zaphon* means "north, to hide and to store, a storage place." That meaning will be profoundly important to us in a moment, so keep note of it in your mind.

The term *high places* comes directly from the Hebrew word *bamah,* and it means, literally, "a high place and heights" (Strong's H1116). Strong's also defines this word to mean "battlefields, the chief places of the land, giving possession, victory, and dominion." Do you see what I see here? The act of worshiping graven images or idols turns the very land of the high place into a battlefield. When the Israelites worshiped these images upon the high places, it became the chief place where the land itself was given into possession of the enemy—and where he obtained victory and dominion over the Israelites. By worshiping idols on a high place, it becomes a governmental handover of authority, which is why it is so important that they are torn down. You see, the enemy has no authority. Jesus took back the keys of authority that always belonged to Him when He went into hell those three days He was in the tomb. So as it stands, satan's authority amounts to *zero*. None. However, he manipulates and steals authority by way of our agreement. When we worship or give place to idols in the high places of our own hearts, we essentially are handing over the keys that Jesus died to give us.

High Places Are Battlefields

In reading the account of Deborah, as well as other stories of battle that the Israelites faced—particularly throughout Judges and then 1 and 2 Kings—you will find that most of the battles that came against God's people began because they either participated in high-place worship or had neglected to remove these high places from their habitations. They opened the very door of idol worship that, in turn, gave way to their own oppression. Worshiping graven, self-made images was and continues to be the highest form of offense to the Lord. Imagine for a moment how it must feel to God to have His children worship graven images? Imagine a child you have conceived, protected in your womb throughout those long nine months, birthed through the hardship of labor, and raised day and night, surrounding and doting on them with all your love and affection, protecting them, feeding them, nourishing them, and teaching them. Now imagine that child were to grow up, find a mere rock on the ground, and turn their back entirely on you, saying, "This rock is my mother. I will give all my affection to this rock, for it birthed me, loves me, and protects me." Imagine they took this rock, gave it a place of prominence in their home, and never invited you back again but instead offered this rock your role in their lives. It would not only be an insult, but it would also be a downright mockery of all the love and care you have provided for that child.

The Israelites did all this and worse, for they then sacrificed their very own infants to these graven rock and gold images. Psalm 106:36-37 (NIV) says, *"They worshiped their idols, which became a snare to them. They sacrificed their sons and their daughters to false gods.*" What's worse, they beat drums to drown out the cries of the infants as they were sacrificed in the flames of the high altars. Jesus had strong words for this practice—so strong, in fact, that He linked one of the main places where this took place to hell—Gehenna, which is where we get our word for "hell" today.

Leading up to the account of Deborah, we read in Judges 2:11-13 (ESV) of Israel's continued unfaithfulness:

> *And the people of Israel did what was evil in the sight of the Lord and served the Baals. And they abandoned the Lord, the God of their fathers, who had brought them out of the land of Egypt. They went after other gods, from among the gods of the peoples who were around them, and bowed down to them. And they provoked the Lord to anger. They abandoned the Lord and served the Baals and the Ashtaroth.*

The Israelites lived in this cycle in which they would worship these idols, God's anger would arise toward them, He would hand them over into the hands of an oppressor, they would cry out to Him for help, He would rescue them, and they would momentarily turn their hearts back toward Him before stumbling back, eyes wide open, into idol worship again.

By the time we get to Deborah's account, we find this same cycle on repeat. In Judges 4:1 (ESV), we are told, *"And the people of Israel **again** did what was evil in the sight of the*

Lord after Ehud died." God raised up judges like Deborah, Gideon, and Samson who were appointed by Him to destroy these high places, call for repentance, and realign the hearts of God's people back toward the Lord. Their roles weren't easy ones, but they were necessary to restore peace in the land and rightful worship to the Lord. Today, as we carry the mantle of Deborah, we face a similar wrestle.

High Places in Our World Today

When we lived in Redding, California during the years of 2020–2022, we would often visit the two mountains that frame the city of Redding—Shasta and Lassen. Their enormous peaks cast a beautiful backdrop for the valley that Redding sits in. Both mountains offer a plethora of outdoor explorations, so many families, including our own, often made the hour or two road trip to their peaks for day visits. On one such visit to Shasta, we had driven up to where the snow covered the heights of the summit, and there was a nice little walking track we could trudge through with our snow boots and explore some of the woods.

As we were walking around the wintry wonderland of freshly fallen snow, I noticed a lady dressed kind of odd for the surroundings. She was wearing a long, draping black dress and a black veil, and I quickly recognized she was performing some kind of ritual just behind the trees. We immediately pled the Blood of Jesus over ourselves, our family, and even the mountain and the city, protecting against any dark or demonic thing she might be engaging with, and then we kept walking on our way. Friends of ours in the city had often told us that Mount Shasta would draw in all kinds of strange visitors, especially those seeking witchcraft worship, as they believe this high mountain holds some kind of spiritual authority. Kind of interesting when you think about it, because as off base as they are, their actions are, to this day, leading back to biblical roots. People are still on the same woeful cycle that the Israelites were.

As strange as it was to see this woman performing actual "high place" idolatry in our day, this isn't the kind of high place worship that mainly concerns us in our world today. While yes, it is still demonic, in many ways it is the least of high place idolatry that we are in a wrestle against. What I mean by that is, there is a far greater plague of "high place" idolatry that has infested the hearts and minds of people of every race, tribe, and tongue. Rather than chasing witches off a mountain, we are engaged against demons of thought that have seduced the entire world in a myriad of ways. Do you remember in the last chapter the verses I mentioned from 2 Corinthians 10:4-6 (NKJV)? Let's revisit them to understand what I mean here.

> *For the weapons of our warfare are not carnal but mighty in God for pulling down strongholds, casting down arguments and every high thing that exalts itself against the knowledge of God, bringing every thought into captivity to the obedience of Christ, and being ready to punish all disobedience when your obedience is fulfilled.*

As I write, I can feel the immense gravity of these words in my spirit and the keys of our authority that they hold to cast

117

down these strongholds of thought. I pray this revelation sits in your heart as heavy as it does mine, for you have been given all authority by Jesus, in heaven and on earth, to trample on these scorpions in high places. The high things, the high places of our day are *thoughts*, *arguments*, and *knowledge*. Everything that sets itself *against* the true knowledge of God in our day and age *is* a high place. In other words, anything that destroys the image of God, anything that comes against His one and only truth, anything that mocks His Son or His Holy Spirit *is* indeed a high place of thoughts and lofty imaginations. These high places aren't difficult to find either. Take abortion, for example. Look how it destroys the knowledge of God as the creator of life. Look how it destroys the knowledge of you and me made *in the image* of God from within the womb. Look how it sacrifices children to its sacrament. The mantra "my body, my choice" is a direct perversion of "His body (Jesus) for my freedom." Abortion says that to have freedom I must murder my infant child in my womb upon the altar of myself. Abortion is a high place.

Notice that satan's high place started in his heart as a form of pride. *"You said in your heart, 'I will* ascend *to the heavens; I will raise my throne* above *the stars of God'"* (Isaiah 14:13 NIV). Pride of self has become the hiding place of high places in the hearts of people, and it's not just through abortion or LGBT, either. A high place is anything that takes the place of God in our hearts, and you and I must not be deceived into thinking that we are immune to the seduction of a high place in our own hearts.

This brings me back to the meaning of Mount Zaphon. Remember the place that lucifer told himself he would sit enthroned in? It means "north, north wind, to hide and to store, a storage place." Why would one of the meanings of Zaphon be "north"? Doesn't "north" speak of heading in the right direction? Well, yes, but in this case, no, because it does not mean "true north." It is important to remember that satan mimics what God has spoken, and he will offer a perverted version of north to any unsuspecting and unprotected mind.

Looking at the ideology of LGBT, you will notice that the foundation for their identity is "love." As a Christian, this is a difficult standpoint to argue against, right? Because Jesus *is* love. So it makes some sense to accept their desire for love, does it not? Only this version of love goes in direct opposition to God's love. It looks as though its north, but it is not true north. For in His love, there can be no lie. Jesus accepted all who came to Him. He loved on and dined with sinners, yes. He would not have turned away one single person from the LGBT community, and He should continue to be our standard today. He loved them and continues to love them today. However, there was a standard of truth and sacrifice that He required for anyone to follow Him, and as such, many walked away.

Do you see how these high places hide as "north"? The enemy hides these exalted thoughts in the hearts of man as his storage place of exaltation, making these thoughts appear to be true, but they are not the one and true north. Similarly, the enemy makes himself to look like a lion in 1 Peter 5:8 (NIV) where it says, *"Be alert and of sober mind. Your enemy the devil prowls around like a roaring lion looking for someone to devour."* Satan will never be the true lion or true north, for no part in him holds any truth. It is important that you can discern the difference. Peter warns us to be alert and of sober mind, which is a warning to keep your thoughts free of intoxication (or drunkenness) of the world's thoughts and ideologies. One surefire way of knowing if you are becoming drunk on worldly ideologies, and therefore setting your heart up as a hidden storage of a high place, is that you agree with everything the world says. In addition, if there is something or someone in your life who has a higher position of affection above God in your heart, you will know that has become a high place, and it's time to tear it down.

Psalm 89:11-13 (NASB) is an incredible passage that ties all of this together:

> *The heavens are Yours, the earth also is Yours; the world and all it contains, You have established them. The north and the south, You have created them; Tabor and Hermon shout for joy at Your name. You have a strong arm; Your hand is mighty, Your right hand is exalted.*

You will notice how these verses mention the high place: "the heavens are Yours"! Both north and south, the high places of the earth, belong to the Creator. You might have noticed, too, the name of Deborah's mountain, Tabor. *"Tabor and Hermon shout for joy at **your name**."* This speaks of taking these high and lofty arguments and setting them *against* the name of Jesus, over whom they cannot prevail. Verse 13 then speaks of the strength of His arm—His right hand is a prophetic picture of victory in battle. Where God is exalted, He fights our battles for us and destroys every exaltation that has come against us. You might remember that Tabor means "to purify and clarify." Well, it also means "a high place," which leads us to the next strategy of Deborah's.

Consecrated

Following on from the next verses in Deborah's account, we know that she had just summoned Barak and instructed him to take their 10,000 men to Mount Tabor to prepare and purify the high place there. We learned how strategic this move was, and considering the importance of high places gives even deeper insight into her acute strategy. Deborah and Barak were facing a powerful enemy from within by the name of Jabin, king of Canaan, who reigned in Hazor and the commander of his army, Sisera, who lived in Harosheth-hagoyim (see Judges 4:2-3). Jabin and Sisera together had cruelly oppressed God's people for 20 years. Even though this oppression came because of the Israelites' own sin through the worship of these idols, God's deliverance and mercy once again were rising to meet them in their distress. First, however, Deborah knew the high places had to be purified, which was why Tabor carried such prophetic significance for this moment. As you can expect from me by now, the names and meanings of Israel's enemies and the locations in which they lived are integral to understanding the battle Deborah faced and, in turn, the one we face today.

The king of Canaan, *Jabin*, means "discerner." Now, Jabin reigned in Hazor, which means a "castle or a village." Remember how names were given in biblical times to represent divine destiny? This tells us that Jabin was called to be a good king over Israel who discerned right from wrong, good from evil. Unfortunately, however, like the kings before him he failed to step into his divine calling, and instead he became a counterfeit of what he was called to do. His discernment was deceived, and he partnered with evil rather than against it. It's amazing to see that the place he reigned in, *Hazor*, means both a castle and a village. It reminds us of the "village life ceasing" from Deborah's song. Village life in Israel became heavily oppressed because they had given themselves over to a high place, which turned their village into a stronghold or a castle. High with its walls and strong with its gates, they were locked in rather than having freedom to move, and they needed a rescuer to come and destroy its foundations.

Now, the commander of his army was Sisera; his name means "meditations" and "keen and swift." Sisera lived in *Harosheth-hagoyim*, which means "silencer of the Gentiles" and "carving of the nations." Sisera represents the meditations of the mind, the high places of thoughts, the strongholds of contemplations. Sisera is a prophetic allegory for the exact same enemy we are in contention with in our world today. The meditations of Sisera are the arguments, the high and lofty thoughts that set themselves up against our God. These meditations of thought and knowledge are the high places that hide themselves within the hearts of men and women as strongholds.

What is fascinating is where Sisera lived—Harosheth-hagoyim. The meditations of idol thoughts gave Sisera permission to "silence the Gentiles," which points to you and me, the

Gentiles of Christianity. Think of the prophetic symbolism of masking in the past few years. It speaks of fear and silencing a voice—masking and holding captive the mouths of you and me, who are meant to be casting down these strongholds with our voices. Sisera's meditations have keenly and swiftly captivated the world. What could "carving the nations" mean though? It speaks of division, of carving idolatrous thoughts, lies, and speech into foundational truths. Sisera is no enemy to be messed with lightly. This enemy must be opposed with fierce courage and divine instruction.

Bringing Every Thought Captive

So how do we pull down this enemy? How do we tear down the idols and altars of high places? How do you and I together, bearing Deborah's mantle, oppose the Sisera of our day? Second Corinthians 10:4-6 tells us that the weapons of our warfare are not carnal. Deborah had supernatural insight for her battle, though hers was physical. We too need divine insight for our battles, though ours is largely spiritual. The weapons we wage war with are found in the Word of God. Having first put on our full armor, we bring every thought captive into the obedience of Christ Jesus. What does that mean, exactly?

The New Living Translation of 2 Corinthians 10:5 explains it like this: "*We destroy every proud obstacle that keeps people from knowing God. We capture their rebellious thoughts and teach them to obey Christ.*" That all might sound good and dandy on paper, but the question remains—how is that done practically, in prayer and action, today? Does this mean we are meant to run into every "high place" and yell and scream at people that they must obey Christ? No. This is done first and foremost in prayer and intercession. Mount Tabor is where you take the lie and cleanse it in the clarifying and purifying Blood of Jesus. Take that high place up here, imagine carrying the thought with you, and call that thought into alignment according to the Word. By doing this, you are taking it captive. Cleanse the thoughts with Jesus and find out what His thoughts are over the things that have raised themselves up against Him. What does He say about your family member who is living a life of sin and who is bound by the high place of drugs, for example—a substance that has set itself against Christ as the answer in their lives? Tear down that high place in prayer by declaring their true love is found in Jesus. Cleanse the thoughts that are waging war against them by surrounding them with the truth of God's promises. Whenever you see this loved one, remind them of their worth. These are all things I have done with loved ones in my life and seen God move powerfully every time.

Truth or Lies?

As I end this chapter, I want to briefly share a very personal story of mine. After my second child Sophie was born, I went through a season of burnout as I was adjusting to raising two children under three. What I didn't know was that the enemy was about to hit me hard in the areas of many lies I had built my life and identity on. One day as I was with the girls as Nate worked, it felt like a dark cloud descended over my head—a dark cloud of lies about my life, my worth, and my ability as a mother, just to name a few. I felt trapped and unable to function, so I called Nate and desperately asked him to come home. When he arrived home, he said it was like I was tormented, which I can see now that I was. Every day I would wake up fine until at some point that dark cloud would descend, and I would have to worship and pray my way out of it. I soon discovered that as I read the truth of the Word of God over myself, the cloud would lift quicker. What was happening? I was in a war over the truth of my identity, and the lies that the enemy had planted in my life were starting to become loosed as I spoke the truth of who I was. It wasn't an easy path. It shook our family and we went through the fire, but one night almost a year after that battle began I received my complete freedom.

This is our charge—to ascend to the high places and take down what has been exalted. Whether in your own life or in your sphere of influence, you have been given an amazing invitation to partner with heaven to set the record straight. It's time to ascend, mighty daughter, and take the high places!

Deborah's Arsenal

Weapon #6: You are Seated in Christ

You have been given authority by the Blood of the Lamb to tear down strongholds—every thought, argument, and high thing that raises itself in opposition to Christ. You do this by remembering that you are anointed and seated in Christ in heavenly places (Ephesians 2:6). To break this down, your spirit is literally seated inside of Christ on the throne, and you have been given His same authority to wield on the earth.

The question is, are you wielding your authority or not? You are not below and under the enemy—like he wants you to feel—but you are above the enemy. You have Christ's authority over every demonic assignment that comes against you or around you. So when you pray, remember where you are seated—*in* Christ—and from there you pray and tear down every demonic plan! Use your authority and position today.

Your Charge: Tear Down Strongholds!

Do you have high places in your own life? Places that you continually keep coming back to again and again?

Speak the Word over this situation and worship through it. No matter how big or small the high place is, if it's one you are dealing with repetitively, learn how to cast it down by declaring God's Word over it.

Write down in your journal some of the strongholds that you see personally in your own life and family. Now take them down in prayer. Do the same with the strongholds you see around in your nation. What needs to come down?

Part Three

THE DEBORAH REVOLT

Chapter Seven

GOD'S WAR PLAN

*"We have taught a generation
to feast and play, but the times
demand that we fast and pray."*
—Lou Engle

"When it rains, it pours." Have you ever heard this phrase or even said it yourself? It is a commonly used idiom for when a bad situation arises and usually other bad things take place all at the exact same time. Have you ever faced a circumstance when everything seems to hit you all at once? If you're alive and breathing, you probably have. Say, for example, your alarm fails to go off for work in the morning and you wake up late and rush to get ready, only to discover you have a flat tire in your car and a dead battery as well. "When it rains, it pours."

Sometimes life will throw everything at us simultaneously when we're off guard. Now, not everything that happens to you will be sent from the enemy—sometimes it's just "life." However, there are times when you know in your spirit, "This is an attack." There are too many unusual and disruptive things happening all at once for this to just be a coincidence, and it can often feel as though you are living that very phrase: "When it rains, it pours." We've had times in our own lives when we have been struggling under the weight of multitudes of circumstances and I have looked at Nate and said, "I feel like I'm drowning. I need to come up for air." In those times, however, I have had to learn how to not find my breath in good circumstances but in the strength and stability of the One who holds me despite them and through them. I love what Bill Johnson says, "If you find yourself in the valley of the shadow of death, keep walking." In other words, don't stay there—keep taking steps of faith; keep moving until the faithful hand of Jesus guides you safely out.

I would like to propose to you that from here on out we're going to flip the meaning of that phrase. I would like to suggest that from now on, "When it rains, it pours," is speaking of a downpour of God, rushing in like a flood to drown out your enemies that are threatening to suffocate you. You might be facing such opposition today—situations that are all too difficult to bear, a myriad of problems that you can't figure out—whether it be loss, disappointment, delay, or betrayal. Know this: He who holds all of creation holds you. If you will lean in and quiet your anxious heart, rest your weary head against the faithful beat of His heart, you will find peace and courage amid your storms. I am reminded of this verse in Isaiah 59:19 (NIV), *"From the west, people will fear the name of the Lord, and from the rising of the sun, they will revere his glory. For he will come like a pent-up flood that the breath of the Lord drives along."*

There has been a lot of controversy surrounding this one verse because it has been wrongly translated or, rather, given incorrect grammar in a critical junction of the verse. Many people are more familiar with this verse like this: *"When the enemy shall come in like a flood, the Spirit of the Lord shall lift up a standard against him"* (KJV).

Numerous biblical scholars have pointed out the incorrect placement of the comma here, concluding that original manuscripts of this scripture read like this: "When the enemy shall come in, *like a flood* the Spirit of the Lord shall lift up a standard against him."

That one little comma changes the entire meaning of this verse. Instead of the flood being attributed to the enemy, the flood is instead correctly attributed to God. Therefore, in our little phrase, "When it rains, it pours," we are going to flip its meaning to attribute the flood to God. You'll see how very soon.

You Prepare a Table Before Me in the Presence of My Enemies

We know that Barak felt somewhat overwhelmed and apprehensive as he prepared to face Sisera and his armies. Even with the promise from God that Israel's enemies would be delivered into his hands, he still had to walk out the battle, and that evidently caused him to feel some reservation. We read this conversation between him and Deborah in Judges 4:8-9 (ESV):

> Barak said to her, "If you will go with me, I will go, but if you will not go with me, I will not go." And she said, "I will surely go with you. Nevertheless, the road on which you are going will not lead to your glory, for the Lord will sell Sisera into the hand of a woman." Then Deborah arose and went with Barak to Kedesh.

How many times have you had conversations like this with the Lord in which you have said, "I just need confirmation. I need to know that You are with me." I love that Deborah did not rebuke Barak for feeling a sense of unease. Instead, she rose to immediately go with him. Despite his trepidations, Barak is listed among the greats of faith in Hebrews 11:32. That's just like our beautiful God, isn't it? Where we remember Barak for his moment of fear and trembling, God remembers Barak for his great faith in action. Where you remember your moments of fear and anxiety, God remembers the moments when you stood up in courage despite your trembling knees. I am intrigued, though—why did Deborah and Barak detour to Kedesh? I thought the Lord's instruction was to rally the troops at Mount Tabor, yet it seems they took a little detour and stopped at Kedesh first on their way to the battle.

As with all of Deborah's story, nothing written here is by mistake. *Kedesh* means "to be holy and consecrated." It also means "sacred place" and "sanctuary." They diverted to Kedesh before Mount Tabor because they needed to be holy and set apart to the Lord before going into battle. It's possible they offered a sacrifice here. It's not written in the Bible that they did, but given the history of the small city of Kedesh, which was known as a place of refuge, it is highly probable that they went there to give thanks to the Lord ahead of the battle as a declaration that He was their refuge in the midst of the coming storm. They also called their troops to Kedesh as well, knowing that the key to winning this war was found in consecration.

> *And Barak called out Zebulun and Naphtali to Kedesh. And 10,000 men went up at his heels, and Deborah went up with him* (Judges 4:10 ESV).

Consecrate comes from the Hebrew word *qadash* and it means, "to be holy, to prepare, to purify" (Strong's H6942). Why was this necessary? It's important to remember, as we read this account of Deborah, that we are reading her story through the lens of the New Testament—in our New Covenant with Jesus, Yeshua. So I believe their offbeat path to Kedesh was a prophetic foreshadow of Deborah and Barak first setting themselves apart, purifying and cleansing themselves from what was behind, and communing with God in His sanctuary. I believe this was a prophetic picture of fasting and prayer.

Someone who has really taught me a lot about the power of fasting through his life is Lou Engle. If there's a crisis or injustice in the world, you can be sure that Lou has stood in prayer and fasted over it at some point. In 2017 while we were at the Dallas prophetic summit, Nate bumped into Lou and had a conversation about fasting. Nate asked Lou for some advice for our generation, to which he responded by beginning to sway back and forth and with a passionate plea: "I pray that your generation would separate themselves to a lifestyle of fasting and prayer!"

Fasting is a lifestyle of consecration to the Lord—a call that goes beyond Sunday worship and YouTube sermons and calls forth God's daughters out of mediocrity into the place of partnership and devotion that shifts the nations. This is the consecration you are called to and the place of strength that is your refuge for your journey.

> "Join a company of young men and women who have made a covenant by sacrifice to turn a nation through united massive fasting and prayer." —Lou Engle

The Power in the Wait

From Kedesh, we find that Deborah, Barak, and his 10,000 men finally made it to the top of Mount Tabor. They were now fully prepared as they sat atop this lookout and waited to see their enemies marching before them. I'm sure it felt a little unnerving waiting to see the strength of the armies marching toward them. What would it feel like as they first saw them appear on the horizon? Intimidating, I'm sure. Did they want to move into immediate action and run toward them? Most likely, but the Lord's instruction was to wait. It was the calm before the storm as they sat patiently watching and waiting until the Lord gave the command through Deborah to move.

The mention of Barak's 10,000 men reminds me, funnily enough, of a nursery rhyme I was taught when I was little. You know the kind of nursery rhyme that you have no idea what it means or what it's about, but you sing it as a child because it has a catchy tune? It was called "The Grand Old Duke of York." The lyrics are:

> Oh, the grand old Duke of York
>
> He had ten thousand men
>
> He marched them up to the top of the hill
>
> And he marched them down again
>
> And when they were up, they were up,
>
> And when they were down, they were down,
>
> And when they were only half-way up
>
> They were neither up nor down.

When I researched the meaning behind this nursery rhyme, I came to discover that it was loosely written about an English duke from the 1400s whose forces of 10,000 men were outnumbered and defeated at the Battle of Wakefield in Northern England in the year of 1460. Those details are not what's integral here, though. This nursery rhyme was said to highlight the duke's futile military actions. In other words, he had no strategy. He looked like he was moving in battle, but really all he was doing was moving his men from place to place. The most they achieved was going up and down, but they were basically going nowhere. There is a lesson to be learned here. Sometimes when we are out of sync with God in battle, we can be like this duke—our strategies can make us look like we are moving in battle, when in reality we aren't either here nor there. Deborah and Barak's army, on the other hand, might have looked futile in the moment, waiting atop a mountain, but they were obediently following clear instruction from the Lord as they waited for His next command. It started when they first positioned themselves in consecration at Kedesh. Because of this time, they had gained the upper hand, and now they waited in rest.

Waiting in God can be the most powerful thing you can do in a battle, but it can also be the most difficult thing. Knowing when to wait and when to move will only be clear to you when, like Deborah, you are found in the secret place of His presence.

> *But they who wait for the Lord shall renew their strength; they shall mount up with wings like eagles; they shall run and not be weary; they shall walk and not faint* (Isaiah 40:31 ESV).

When the Lord first called me to pray to see the end of abortion—specifically, to pray to see the fall of Roe v. Wade—it was some 12 years ago now. Waiting on God to see the final fulfilment of that prayer was no easy task. (It was mere months ago at the time of this writing. I still find myself in awe.) Watching, waiting, anticipating as, from a distance, I could see the strength of our foes, and I had to continually find myself waiting on the Lord for renewed strength. It is that battle, though, that has strengthened me for others.

Now, Deborah and Barak and their troops waited, and in their waiting their enemies were alerted to their position. Judges 4:12-13 (ESV) says, *"When Sisera was told that Barak the son of Abinoam had gone up to Mount Tabor, Sisera called out all his chariots, 900 chariots of iron, and all the men who were with him, from Harosheth-hagoyim to the river Kishon."* It's interesting, really, that Sisera was not told of their movements when they went to Kedesh. Ten thousand men moving together is no small sight to behold, yet it wasn't then that he was alerted—it was when they were waiting atop Mount Tabor that he was told. It's almost as if God purposely allowed it that way. He wanted to lure him in, and like a moth to a flame Sisera came.

Fail to Prepare, You Prepare to Fail

I want you to close your eyes and picture yourself standing atop Mount Tabor alongside Deborah, Barak, and 10,000 others. Fully dressed in your armor, you and your fellow soldiers are eerily quiet, for there is a stillness that has collectively descended upon the mountain top as you await the approach of your enemy. All that can be heard is the hushed breath of you and your company. Suddenly, in the far distance, a cloud of dust can be seen rising above the horizon, and you know it is the feet of Sisera, his iron chariots and multitudes stirring up the earth as they march toward you. Do you feel angst and fear? Or do you feel resolve? Do you calculate in your mind the sheer numbers and strength of Sisera's battalion against the mere 10,000 of your own? Or do you rehearse the promise God has spoken through the prophet Deborah?

In the reality of our own lives, daughters, this is where many of us sadly retreat. We see the sheer force, "strength," and numbers of the approaching enemy, which today could represent a myriad of things. Take censorship on social media, for example. Do I retreat from speaking the truth merely because the social media giants attempt to silence me into submission? Do I water down the Gospel and every moral foundation merely to appease the screaming mobs, all because what I am saying does not align with their ideologies? Or do I continue to blaze forward, unafraid, knowing the strength of the One in whose promises I fight? I want you to sincerely ask yourself this question, because it is a question we must all answer at some point in our lives. "Would I retreat in the day of battle if I saw a menacing army approaching me?"

That question might be a little too easy to answer because it's one thing to imagine it, but it's another thing to walk it out. So ask yourself this, "Have I retreated in the past? Have I been overwhelmed at the magnitude of opposition in my own personal life and wondered, 'How could I possibly engage in a battle bigger than the ones I am contending with right now?'" I get it. I really do. However, daughter, this is the moment to which you have been called. Therefore, it is not a moment you can retreat from. If your boots (or heels) aren't dug into the ground now, you will shake and tremble at the sight of an incoming enemy, and you'll likely run if your foundation isn't strong.

On the other hand, if you take heed now and firmly secure your foundation in what God has said in this moment before the battle, you will be immovable on the day of battle. Your knees won't be trembling at the mere sight of an intimidating enemy; you will be locked in to the eyes of Jesus, knowing and trusting that He is the One who will win the battle for you and through you. However, your victory isn't won solely on the battlefield itself; it's won in the preparation. As we learned previously about the Aussie rugby team, they failed to prepare, and therefore they prepared to fail. Your preparations, the little moments in your day when you set aside time for God, when you choose to make sure you are spending daily time in the Word and in His presence, are the little moments that will matter when you face the big moments. Are you feeling fearful today? Are you finding yourself wavering at the battles you are facing in your own life? Are you retreating on what God has said? It's time to strengthen yourself in the Lord. I am reminded of these verses from Isaiah 35:3-7 (ESV):

> *Strengthen the weak hands, and make firm the feeble knees. Say to those who have an anxious heart, "Be strong; fear not! Behold, your God will come with vengeance, with the recompense of God. He will come and save you." Then the eyes of the blind shall be opened, and the ears of the deaf unstopped; then shall the lame man leap like a deer, and the tongue of the mute sing for joy. For waters break forth in the wilderness, and streams in the desert; the burning sand shall become a pool, and the thirsty ground springs of water;*

in the haunt of jackals, where they lie down, the
grass shall become reeds and rushes.

I love the fruit that comes from trusting in God: *"the eyes of the blind will be opened, the ears of the deaf unstopped."* The blind and the deaf are indeed speaking of the natural inabilities to see and hear, but they are also a prophetic allegory for opening the eyes and ears of the spiritually blind—those who are blinded by the god of this world. When your hand and heart are strengthened in the Lord, it makes way for God to move, as opposed to your fear becoming a stumbling block that inhibits what He is wanting to do.

Then, in verses 6-7, we see something amazing happens. Miraculous waters gush forth in the wilderness, and streams pour out in the desert. Consider with me for a moment just what a miracle this is implying. Here in Australia, we are known for our "sun-drenched" land—18 percent of our entire land mass is made up entirely of desert, yet some 35 percent of our land rarely receives any rain. It is so dry that it is practically considered desert too. That's a huge portion of dry land when you take into account the sheer size of Australia. Now imagine how miraculous it would be if there were sudden rainfalls that caused streams to flow where there were once endless plains of barren, dry ground. This is what happens to a dry and thirsty land when God's sons and daughters strengthen themselves in Him—a cataclysmic chain reaction takes place. He responds with the rain of His glory, He washes away the invading enemies, He causes those who were blind and deaf to see and hear, and He pours out rivers of living water for the parched and weary. This is what God wants to do through you, daughter, and we're about to see how this is what God was about to do through Deborah and Barak. You might be asking, practically speaking, "How do I do this? Do I strengthen myself in the Lord?" We find another key hidden in Judges 5:11, written in Deborah's song.

> *To the sound of the musicians at the watering places, there they repeat the righteous triumphs of the Lord, the righteous triumphs of his villagers in Israel. Then down to the gates marched the people of the Lord* (ESV).

They repeated God's words, His promises, and what He had done in the past. They rehearsed the voice of the Lord. Notice they did this at the watering places, which suggests, prophetically, that it was in their places of greatest thirst and dire need that they rehearsed who God was and what He had done. Worship is a profound battle key in warfare—to remind yourself and repeat who God is and what He has done. This gave Deborah and Barak the upper hand in a battle that naturally appeared all but lost. This positioned them for victory before the battle even began.

The God Trap

As Sisera marched his multitudes toward Deborah and Barak, I can just about imagine what he was thinking: "This is going to be easy. Look at the sheer strength of my numbers. Look at my iron chariots. I'm going to crush them with one foul blow." The stark contrast between his attitude and Deborah's and Barak's is a testament of where each of their faiths rested. Sisera's faith was in his numbers, in his 900 iron chariots, in what he could tangibly see, in the fortified strength of his army and the previous battles he had won through them. Sisera's faith was in himself. Deborah and Barak held their firm strength in God alone. Their faith was not resting in their own ability but in the promise of what God had said. Their faith was in the invisible army that surrounded theirs. Sisera's faith was in his man-made chariots; Deborah's faith was in God.

The Hebrew word used to describe Sisera's troops is the word *hamon* (Strong's H1995). It defines "a tumultuous crowd of abundance, a great quantity." It is also said to be "a noise, a loud rumbling, and a roar." Sisera's army depicts the noise, the *qol*, of our enemy today. This leads me back to the question, "Where does your faith rest today, daughter?" Is it in your own abilities? Is it in the confidence of what you can or cannot do? Or is your faith securely steadfast in God? Do you rehearse the sheer size and magnitude of your opposing enemy, do you listen to the noisy taunts of the enemy, or do you rehearse the supernatural strength of the God who created the entire earth and the skies above? Do you rehearse the voice, the *qol*, of the serpent, or are you leaning in to the voice, the *qol*, of God in warfare?

It may be difficult to keep your ears tuned to the voice of God in a time when all around you is filled with the sound of a loud, boisterous, and menacing army that is clamoring at your walls and threatening to knock down your gates. I can just hear it now—the simultaneous drum of Sisera's army's feet, the clinking of the armor of his tens of thousands as they march closer and closer. The beat of thousands of horses' hooves, the whips of the drivers, the loud hum of the chariot wheels, the unified voices of the army as they respond to their commander. Sisera's army was a loud and uproarious noise, and today we face a similar tumultuous noise. Social media has become the gates of the world where matters are contended and disputed. At those gates are the deafening screams and demands of submission. If you don't submit to the ideologies and high places of the multitudes, you are threatened to be beat, bruised, and whipped with vicious words and vitriol or silenced if you refuse to bow. Sisera's iron chariots represent prophetically the strength of man, the ideas of man, satanic dominion, and harsh judgment. Iron chariots in the Old Testament paint for us the modern-day allegory of man's works, which ultimately leads to man's ideas and ideologies. High places. The confidence of "self." The armies we face today are spoken of in 2 Timothy 3:2-5 (NKJV):

> *For men will be lovers of themselves, lovers of money, boasters, proud, blasphemers, disobedient to parents, unthankful, unholy, unloving, unforgiving, slanderers, without self-control, brutal, despisers of good, traitors, headstrong, haughty, lovers of pleasure rather than lovers of God, having a form of godliness but denying its power. And from such people turn away!*

This is the modern-day army of Sisera we are facing—a world in love with themselves, in which their faith is in their own strength, they are prideful and arrogant, slanderers of truth and righteousness. Little do they know, however, that it is their pride that will be their downfall. As Sisera was about to find out, the very confidence he had in himself was leading him and his army right into an unsuspected trap.

Sisera's army gathered at the River Kishon, unable to climb the heights of Mount Tabor due to his iron chariots. He instructed his army to lie in wait at the foot of the mountain. God's next instruction came through Deborah as she prophesied to Barak and the ten thousand:

> *"Up! For this is the day in which the Lord has delivered Sisera into your hand. Has not the Lord gone out before you?" So Barak went down from Mount Tabor with ten thousand men following him. And the Lord routed Sisera and all his chariots and all his army with the edge of the sword before Barak; and Sisera alighted from his chariot and fled away on foot* (Judges 4:14-15 NKJV).

Now to give you some perspective, as Barak and his men came down the mountain, the Lord routed the battle to a nearby town, tiny in size, called Taanach, which was located alongside the waters of Megiddo, as depicted in Judges 5:19 (ESV): "*The kings came, they fought; then fought the kings of Canaan, at Taanach, by the waters of Megiddo; they got no spoils of silver.*" These two battle locations, as small and insignificant as they may appear, held profound significance for the victory over this menacing army. The tiny town of Taanach, merely 14 acres large, means "He that humbles, He that answers." The Lord led the enormous numbers of Barak's army into a small space to display the sheer greatness of His abilities. God chooses to use the weak things to shame the strong (see 1 Corinthians 1:27). He led them into a place of humbling where they would first begin to witness the battle turning away from their favor as the Lord began to answer His people. Then, by the waters of Megiddo, He routed them once more. *Megiddo* means "the place of multitudes" and "exposure." The Lord led the multitudes of His enemies into a land of exposure before they died by the sword there. Finally, what remained of the iron chariots, Sisera's impressive strength, his pride, and his faith in himself was in the end led down to the river Kishon. *Kishon* means "the place of snaring, a hard and sore place." There, the Lord sent a mighty, torrential rain that would cause the river to swell and, as Judges 5:21 (ESV) describes: *"The torrent Kishon swept them away, the ancient torrent, the torrent Kishon."*

The Lord laid a trap for the enemies of Israel and washed them away. "When it rains, it pours." The Lord used their very pride and trust in themselves and laid a trap to snare them through their own arrogance. Today, the Lord is doing the same through you and me. The snare of our enemy is his own pride. As you and I humble ourselves before the Lord and worship Him in the midst of raging armies that threaten to destroy us on every side, the Lord shall lift up a standard against them. Now, just to reiterate, I am speaking of spiritual enemy forces. Though it often does feel as though we are waging war against humans, we need to keep our eyes on the things above. We need to keep our eyes engaged on who God is and what He has promised. As we do, we will see the demon forces that have entrapped and enslaved entire generations before us ensnared and washed away in the rivers of His living water. We will see generations set free from the enemies of thought; we will see the blind receive their sight again, and the deaf will be able to hear. They will all look and say, "I see Him, I see the King of Glory" as the chains of their captivity will be broken.

We are not waging war against people—we are waging war for their freedom, for their salvation. When you remember who your enemy is, it won't be as difficult to drown out the noise of satan's threats and taunts. You'll remember this isn't personal—this is eternal. You will be able to say with confidence, "When it rains, it pours," knowing that the Lord is about to pour out His Spirit as never before upon a generation of sons and daughters alike. They are mantled with Deborah's anointing to drive out enemy forces before them and watch as the torrents of His outpouring wash them away. This, daughter, is the hour to dig your heels in and remind yourself of what God has said. This, daughter, is the hour of victory as God exposes the multitudes of thought and ideologies that have kept our generations spellbound. This is the hour of cleansing and purification. "When the enemy shall come in, *like a flood* the Spirit of the Lord shall lift up a standard against him."

Living Under His Banner

As I end this chapter, I feel there is an applicable truth you need to digest and deeply be acquainted with. The word *standard* in Isaiah 59:19 means "to display, make to flee, to put to flight, hide, or to cause to escape." It is both a means of rescue and safety as well as a proclamation of God's power and protection, which is why some versions of the Bible use the word banner instead. Imagine for a moment if God raised a physical banner like this over you everywhere you went. It would strike fear and awe into the hearts of those who saw it and cause you to live in a whole new level of confidence that He is for you and helping you every step of the way. Today, daughter, I feel the Lord wanting you to know that He is that banner over you, brooding over you, covering you, and leading you. In God's war plan, the skill and strength isn't dependent on you but on the One who overshadows you. All you need to do is stay under His wings.

Deborah's Arsenal

Weapon #7: The Power of the Holy Spirit

Daughter, the battles you are facing—and those you will face in the days to come—won't be won by your giftings, abilities, or your strength but by the power of His Holy Spirit. You are not alone in your battles; you have the promise of His Spirit right at your side at every moment. The giants in the land look powerful, menacing, and prideful as they oppose God. They parade around in their apparent victories, but God has the last laugh because He is the only real contender.

What am I saying? Your greatest weapon is always found in your relationship with the Holy Spirit. As you engage with Him through your surrender and yield to Him—instead of trying to fight in your own might—you will see the strength of His presence rise up within you.

How do you do this? Learn to move *with* the Holy Spirit, learn the rhythms of His voice, learn to still and quiet your soul when all around you is raging, and listen for His still, small voice. His voice may be quiet in the midst of adversity, yet when you lean in and listen, His voice becomes the loudest roar—a roar so ferocious it instills fear in the enemy's camp.

Your Charge: The Power of His Spirit

You might remember that I shared this following promise in your charge a few chapters back. I want to revisit it again here:

> *Then he answered and spake unto me, saying, This is the word of the Lord unto Zerubbabel, saying, Not by might, nor by power, but by my spirit,' saith the Lord of hosts* (Zechariah 4:6 KJV).

Notice that the Lord is reiterating that the might and strength of man holds nothing compared to His Spirit. His Holy Spirit *is* where your power lies. If you don't have a relationship with Him yet, I encourage you to get yourself a copy of the book *Good Morning, Holy Spirit* by Benny Hinn. This book was revolutionary for my husband and me in understanding the person of the Holy Spirit.

Your charge is to cultivate your relationship with the person of the Holy Spirit, and I can promise you this—your life will *never* be the same. You will see the power of His strength overcoming every battle in your life, leading you and guiding you through every valley and up to the mountaintops.

Chapter Eight

NO MAN'S LAND

"The dogs of doom stand at the doors of your destiny. When you hear them barking you know you are near your promise land. Most people retreat in fear instead of crossing over and capturing their land. Fear is often disguised as wisdom or stewardship but it is a Trojan Horse sent in to steal your destiny. Fear is not your friend!"
—KRIS VALLOTTON

Between the years of 1914–1918, a muddy, narrow, and treeless stretch of wasteland became the battleground for some of the First World War's most gruesome battles. This space of land bore the widely known name, "No Man's Land," which describes an unoccupied space of territory between opposing forces. During the First World War, "No Man's Land" became a bloodied ground of death that lasted years, with "no man" or army able to conquer the territory that lay between. During this time, the German forces and the French-British allies built labyrinths of trenches within this battle zone in an attempt to shield their soldiers from the extreme danger of this territory. The trenches themselves, however, offered little to no protection. In fact, soldiers were subjected to some of the harshest of conditions during their tenure there. If they didn't die from shelling, they faced health dangers. Unsanitary conditions mixed with extreme cold and ongoing dampness often resulted in a condition called "trench foot," which would lead to gangrene and amputation. These conditions were only worsened by the presence of corpses, which lay where they fell in the ditches, sometimes for weeks on end. This of course attracted a plague of large, oversized rats, which in turn caused the spread of multiple diseases as they brazenly took bites out of sleeping, weary soldiers as they rested amidst the chaos. Lice infestations were common too, causing what was known as "trench fever" with a myriad of symptoms such as headaches, fevers, and muscle pain. Not to mention scarcity of food weakened the already immune-deficient soldiers. Then there was the daily reality of imminent and probable death by random shelling, machine gun attacks, and unexpected sniper strikes. I can't even imagine the physical and mental toll these poor soldiers endured.

Now, I know you likely didn't expect to open this book today and be met with such a sad and gruesome description of this history. However, I felt led by the Holy Spirit to high-light their plight for a reason, which we will come back to very soon. No Man's Land reminds me of a scene by the same name in the movie *Wonder Woman*, depicting, with some obvious creative license, their own version of this disputed territory. Allow me to first disclaim about this movie that I am not sug-gesting we are "goddesses," as is the basis of the storyline of the movie. In fact, let me say this with extreme clarity so no one assumes otherwise: we are *not* goddesses. We are made in the image of God, but we are daughters of the Most High. I do not and am not suggesting that we are gods unto ourselves. While we carry the mantle of Deborah, it is solely to *represent* Jesus, not to glorify Deborah or any of us. By sharing this scene, I want to make clear that I am not drawing the conclusion that the mantle of Deborah is remotely like a goddess. The mantle of Deborah is a representation of Jesus. So please hear me when I say I am highlighting this scene alone, entirely sep-arate from the "goddess" narrative, because I believe this one scene holds a prophetic visual of what God's daughters look like on the battlefield.

With that said, if you haven't watched this scene, I highly recommend you put a bookmark on this page and go watch it before reading on. It is titled "No Man's Land, Wonder Woman" on video streaming sites. As you watch, I want you to picture yourself moving out of the trenches and onto that battlefield with the armor of God on. (Maybe a little more appropriately dressed, I might add, with a full set of armor and not such a short skirt. Yes, yes, I'm a prude.) Take a moment to watch the scene, then we'll reconvene.

Know Your Assignment

Welcome back! If you happened to watch the scene, I want to ask you a few questions. Did you cry? Did you feel a sense of courage as you watched it? How did you feel when she climbed the ladder onto the battle scene? What was the component that was most moving to you? For those who did not watch or were unable to for some reason, allow me to briefly explain what occurs. Feel free to skip ahead of this explanation if you watched.

Diana, a.k.a. Wonder Woman, is trekking through battle-grounds led by her guides and companions, with the focus to get to the fiercest point of the battle, at her own request. She is moved by conviction to find the enemy himself so that she can destroy him and, therefore, end the war. Along the way, however, she is deeply stirred and grieved by the scenes of battle that they are passing by, and every time she moves to engage, she is reminded, "This is not your battle. We must keep moving." As they enter the trenches of "No Man's Land," a mother with a child on her lap—both muddied and ragged, sitting deserted in the trenches—desperately grabs a hold of Diana's arm. Hysterically, she describes the dire situation they are in—her home has been captured, women and children are dying, and those who could not escape the village have become enslaved. Diana is moved with compassion and realizes she must stop here and do something. This is where her closest companion attempts to stop her: "This is not what we came here to do!" he exclaims.

Diana turns around, puts on her crown, and turns and says, "No, but it is what I came to do." At that moment, she climbs up the ladder with her shield and emerges onto the barren wasteland. Shots begin to fire at her, which she deflects, as she begins running toward the battle line, deflecting bullets and bombs as she runs. The imagery of the middle of the battlefield is my favorite illustration of warfare. Holding up her shield, she bends down behind it with a storm of fire pummeling against her, deflected off her shield all around her. It is then that her friends run to join her on the field, and together they take the enemy line and eventually reclaim the village that was enslaved.

I have personally watched that scene at least hundreds of times, and my reaction is the same in every single instance—I bawl. When I first saw the movie, a friend and I went together, and I literally had to hold myself back from ugly crying in the cinema. I'm not exaggerating. I held my jacket over my face to stop myself from howling, because honestly, wails were wrestling to burst out of me. I felt so embarrassed and surprised at just how strong the tears flowed; I was not expecting it at all. When driving home that night, I remember asking the Lord, "What was that? Where did that emotion erupt from and why?"

I heard Him reply, "I wanted you to see how I see you on the battlefield. Every time you fight with My Word, every time you hold your ground in the spirit, you are deflecting those arrows with your shield of faith. Every time you run toward the enemy that I have called you to confront, you are taking back disputed territory."

I noticed something interesting too, when the scene was eventually shared on social media. I read through a number of the comments to see if I was alone in my reaction. To my amazement, almost every woman mentioned how they burst into tears. It seemed the reaction was the same with women all over the world. Why? Because it stirs within the heart of every daughter, whether she knows the Lord yet or not, the intrinsic design that God has placed within her. The Father has designed His daughters to be both warriors and nurturers. When many women saw that scene for the first time, their spirits were awakened to the divine call of who God made them to be. Many even wrote, "It felt spiritual," without truly understanding what had been stirred within them. Whether you cried or did not, I am certain that it stirred your spirit within you.

I wanted to highlight something else about this scene. It was women, children, and those enslaved who stirred Diana to move onto the battlefield despite her companions telling her that this was not her fight. It was her closest friend, the one she loved, Trevor, who told her, "This is impossible, Diana, this is not your fight." Yet she instinctively knew that this was indeed her fight and she had to do something. How many times have you been told, "This is not your fight! Stay out of it. You don't have what it takes"? Usually, you will hear these words from those closest to you. Some of the greatest discouragement in my own life has come from the closest of friends and family. Or maybe no one has ever told you this directly, but perhaps you've thought it. You have felt the call of destiny but wondered if you truly have what it takes, and the fear of failure has kept you restrained. How many times have you erased yourself out of the story that God has written for you because you have listened to the ill advice of your company or your fears? Don't get me wrong—I'm not saying you need to wage a war against your friends and family who discourage you, but sometimes you're going to have to turn aside and follow the call. I love what Diana does in this scene. She disputes her stand with her companions for a moment before finally turning aside, saying, "No, this is what I'm going to do."

Not everyone will understand your assignment, and that's okay. If you are feeling the intense gravitational pull from the Holy Spirit to move out of the trenches and onto the battlefield, there will come a moment when you will have to turn aside from the advice of others and follow the voice, the *qol* of God. I can't tell you the number of times I've had friends, family, and those closest to me tell me that I was crazy for interceding to see Roe v. Wade fall. "It's impossible; that's a giant that will never fall; you should devote yourself to something more realistic." I've even had fellow believers in Christ tell me, "We have already prayed sufficiently over this and we have not seen any change. You just need to give it into God's hands and maybe focus on something else." Or worse, "You're not praying God's heart for this." I have been ostracized from prayer groups because of my passion for this call and even asked to leave women's Bible study groups. Not because I was "Bible-bashing" anyone with the message. I learned very early on to tread wisely with how I approached this calling. However, I found that because of the sensitivity and enormity of the topic, no one ever wanted to talk about it. Ever. Let alone pray over it. Sadly, I was often cast out as I could not move from this assignment to which God had called me. As I write this, I have witnessed this "impossible" giant of the law of Roe v. Wade fall to the ground just four months ago. I am here to tell you that what looked impossible to man is possible to God, and I am a witness of His power over these mountains. I know there are battles that still lie ahead, but I can tell you with great confidence from experience that if God has called you to it, you are equal to the task.

Turn Aside

Here in Australia, we have a cultural mindset known as "tall poppy syndrome" that stems back to our convict roots as a nation. I've written about this in my first book, but I felt compelled by the Holy Spirit to share this again. You might be familiar with it, or if you're Australian you will know exactly what I am speaking about. Tall poppy syndrome is a cultural phenomenon in Australia that refers to the mass mindset here. Poppy flowers grow together, and one should not rise above the other. If a poppy gets too tall, it is to be cut down to size, usually by harsh words and condemnation, and sometimes through sarcasm. Nate and I have found ourselves butting against this mentality more often than we would like. We have noticed it particularly in moments of warfare, when we know God is calling us out onto a battlefield to confront or take down a giant. In those moments, the tall poppy syndrome will rear its nasty head. It comes through the voices of friends, family, and even those in ministry. We've had ministry leaders in Australia under the influence of this mindset—which I have come to understand is a deceptive spirit—tell us that we need to restrain ourselves. They have said, "Don't be so bold, tone yourselves down a little, you're coming on too strong."

What I once thought was unique to Australia alone is, in fact, a spiritual mind battle that occurs in defining moments of your destiny regardless of your physical location. This spirit sees you moving onto the battlefield to take back territory that God has called you to, and it tries to cut you down before you get there. I shared a quote at the beginning of this chapter by Kris Vallotton that I want you to read again in light of this mentality:

> The dogs of doom stand at the doors of your destiny. When you hear them barking you know you are near your promise land. Most people retreat in fear instead of crossing over and capturing their land. Fear is often disguised as wisdom or stewardship but it is a Trojan Horse sent in to steal your destiny. Fear is not your friend. —KRIS VALLOTTON

I must stress that I am in no way suggesting your friends or family members are dogs. It is a parabolic description of the enemy barking loudly, often through those closest to you, right at the pivotal moment you are called to cross over. The advice often comes across as "wisdom," but if you will look closely it is laced with fear and condemnation. I once had a family member tell me that I was like a hot air balloon—I was prideful and arrogant because I was rising too far above the clouds with God-dreams. They then told me they were the one standing on the ground shooting arrows at my balloon to bring me back down to earth. This was said about Nate and me starting our ministry, our dreams for what God wanted to do in us, and my prayers over Roe v. Wade to see the giant fall.

This was a "turn aside" moment for me. I had to search my heart with the Father and remind myself of what He had said about me. I knew my family member wasn't intending to partner with the noise and the intimidation of the enemy, but I had to still my heart and attune my ears to the still, small voice, the *only* voice that matters. I asked the Lord, genuinely seeking reproof from Him if I needed it, "Am I being prideful and arrogant for pursuing what You have called me to do?" I remember seeing a clear vision in that instant—I saw my little hot air balloon rising far above the range of those arrows. The arrows were still flying to hit me, but they were falling far beneath the elevation I had floated to, and I knew then I had to turn aside from their words. I chose to forgive this family member for their intent and continued to love them, but I could not allow their words to deter me from moving in the assignment that I knew God had called me to. That was a pivotal moment for me. I remember feeling as though their ropes of opinion that had tied me down were instantly cut loose from restraining me any longer. We find that David faced this same challenge.

When David came to the battlefront and the divine call of the Lord arrested him with a righteous anger against Goliath and the Philistines, David asked those around him, "What will be done for the man who kills Goliath?" Here is how his brother, Eliab, responded to that simple question.

When Eliab, David's oldest brother, heard him speaking with the men, he burned with anger at him and asked, "Why have you come down here? And with whom did you leave those few sheep in the wilderness? I know how conceited you are and how wicked your heart is; you came down only to watch the battle" (1 Samuel 17:28 NIV).

Eliab was moving in this tall poppy syndrome and rose to cut him down. David responded, *"Now what have I done? ... Can't I even speak?"* (1 Samuel 17:29 NIV). This implies that David had been confronted with this mentality before, it wasn't the first time, and because it wasn't his "first rodeo," so to speak, he had obviously learned what to do. In 1 Samuel 17:30 (NIV) it says, *"He then turned away to someone else and brought up the same matter, and the men answered him as before."*

If David had not turned away from his brother's accusations, the historic story between him and Goliath would likely never have taken place and consequently been told throughout the ages.

Discern the Giant You Are Called To

Just like David, you are going to have to learn to discern which voices you are listening to so that you are not distracted from the battlefield you are called to. David could have easily engaged in an argument with his brother Eliab that would have diverted him from the giant he was destined to take down. In the same way, we are about to find out, Jael in the story of Deborah was faced with a similar predicament. While scripture does not give us a whole lot of backstory about Jael, the Bible does offer some key details about her. She was married to Heber, the Kenite, who in Judges 4:11, we are told, was separated from his people. Separation and consecration led by the Holy Spirit for a time is a journey the Lord seems to take us all through. However, isolation from community is another thing. We all will endure seasons of isolation in our lives; it's what we do with those seasons that matters. Sometimes those seasons are led by God, and it seems that Heber was indeed led by God to be separated for a time, consecrated unto Him. However, we find one critical detail about Jael's husband, and it is found in Judges 4:17 (ESV):

> *But Sisera fled away on foot to the tent of Jael,*
> *the wife of Heber the Kenite, for there was peace*
> *between Jabin the king of Hazor and the house*
> *of Heber the Kenite.*

Why is this important? Heber was at peace with Jabin, the king who had cruelly and harshly oppressed the Israelites for 20 long years. It appears that Heber's separation did not lead him closer to the Lord, but further from Him. Maybe he listened to the wrong voices? To be at peace with an enemy meant that there was some form of alliance here. Did the isolation cause him to discern incorrectly? There is a key for us to learn here, especially if you are going through a similar season—make sure it's leading you closer to Jesus, not further from Him.

So where does that leave Jael? While scripture does tell us that the peace agreement extended to Heber's entire household, Jael's actions tell us that there was conflict within her for her husband's alliance. I am not suggesting going against your husband here; what I am saying is Jael chose conviction to the Lord over man's alliances.

> *And Jael came out to meet Sisera and said to him, "Turn aside, my lord; turn aside to me; do not be afraid." So he turned aside to her into the tent, and she covered him with a rug* (Judges 4:18 ESV).

Consider what was at stake for Jael. She would have been familiar with the evil and violent workings of this king, for he was famous for his cruelty, yet peace for her household meant agreement with evil. To directly oppose King Jabin would most likely have jeopardized her husband and her entire family and, in all probability, put their own lives on the line. Kings in Jael's day did not hesitate to hang on the gallows those who opposed them or cut them down by the sword. I'm certain that all this was on her mind when the king's strongest ally showed up right on the doorstep of her tent. Was there conflict within her? Possibly, but she knew what was at stake. Jael had to turn aside from her own fears—fears of what her husband might say, fears of what it might cost her and her family. She had to turn aside from them, and then turn to the Lord. She said to Sisera, "Turn aside. Turn aside to me." This was a "turn aside" moment for Jael. She had to turn aside from the possible tormenting fears and then ask all of Israel's fiercest enemy to turn aside to her, face to face. This was calculated.

The Hebrew word used for *turn aside* in this text is the word *sur*, and it means "to behead, to abolish, to depose of, to strip away, to turn aside off one's course" (Strong's H5493). Why did Sisera not recognize what she was really saying here? The answer is hidden within the deep trenches of his pride. Proverbs 16:18 (ESV) says, *"Pride goes before destruction, a haughty spirit before a fall."* And Proverbs 16:9 (ESV) says, *"The heart of man plans his way, but the Lord establishes his steps."* Pride blinded him from seeing the trap that lay before him. Could it be that the haughtiness of Sisera's heart was the very thing that led him to Jael? Did pride guide his steps there? I believe so. Exhausted from the gaping wounds of a bruised ego, Sisera was in shock, bewildered at the unexpected loss of his powerful army (which he cowardly deserted, by the way). Sisera stumbled into the tent of a woman, the least likely threat on his radar. I can picture him mumbling under his breath, "What could a woman do to *me?*" Little did he know, God uses the least likely to carry out His plans and to annihilate the prideful and powerful. God is not concerned with the world's perceptions on what a powerful warrior is; He looks at the heart. Within Jael's heart, He saw a woman who would choose Him in a consequential moment for Israel. God saw Jael and Jael turned to Him. The Lord chooses the humble in spirit to rest His mighty power upon.

Daughter, have people told you that you are not enough? Have friends discouraged you from stepping into the calling that you know God has anointed you for? Have loved ones kept you in the trenches when you belong on the battlefield? If the harsh words of loved ones and friends have held you in the trenches—if accusations, assumptions, condemnations, and fear of man have held you restrained from the battle to which you have been called—it's time to turn aside. If you feel as though you have never conquered the disputed territory you were called to, it's time to turn aside to the Lord and move in the direction of *His voice* and His voice alone. What is it He has said? What giant has He called you to confront head-on? What enemy are you appointed to throw down? What territory has God anointed you to take back? Because if you stay in the trenches, you'll die there. You were not called to be a trench soldier, hiding within the barricades of accusations, bitten with condemnation, suffering from the scum of tall poppy syndrome, and dying from the shelling of the fear of man. You, daughter, have been anointed, appointed, and called, before you were even born, to run onto battlefields armed with the Spirit of God, to take down the giants that lay before you. Now is the time to come up higher, daughter, come out from there. It is your time to occupy the territory that the enemy has laid waste to and drive a nail into his coffin.

Deborah's Arsenal

Weapon #8: Knowing Who the Father Says You Are

There is no replacement for the voice of the Father in your life. His voice matters more than you may realize in defining moments of destiny—especially when the enemy tries to distract you off course. It's those moments when you are about to swing your sword to take down a giant that you will hear the enemy throwing every lie under his belt at you.

The only thing that will stop you from crumbling under the weight of his accusations and intimidations is the voice of the

Father. Notice, for example, that when David faced Goliath he faced these very intimidations—right at the threshold of one of his greatest victories. David's response was not one of reaction; instead, he reminded himself—and Goliath—whose authority he was standing on. He said, *"I come against you in the name of the Lord Almighty, the God of the armies of Israel, whom you have defied"* (1 Samuel 17:45 NIV). David knew who the Father said he was—he knew his strength was not found in himself but in God—and there on the battlefield he swung his sling and released his stone, standing in the faith of who God said he was.

The Charge: The Weapon of God's Word

Have you dealt with the voice of the enemy trying to stop you from fulfilling the call of God on your life? Maybe the enemy's voice has come through those closest to you, or perhaps it's been the thoughts you hear in your mind. Have you found when you step out that you face opposition from friends, family, and others?

In your journal write down the words and accusations that often come whenever you step out and follow God. Now, open the scriptures and ask the Holy Spirit to give you a weapon for each of those accusations. For example, maybe you're just 19 years old reading this book and you recognize that the enemy is constantly intimidating you with the lie that you are too young. A weapon of God's Word for this lie could be found in Jeremiah 1:6-8 (BSB):

> *"Ah, Lord God," I said, "I surely do not know how to speak, for I am only a child!" But the Lord*

*told me: "Do not say, 'I am only a child.' For to
everyone I send you, you must go, and all that I
command you, you must speak. Do not be afraid
of them, for I am with you to deliver you."*

Find the words of God that destroy the lies and accusations
coming against you, and every time you hear those lies remind
satan of God's truth over you—that you stand in the name of
the Lord and what He has said about you. You have a choice
today to bend to accusations of the naysayers or to move forward regardless of how foolish you look—trusting in who you
are in Christ. The Lord is saying over you today, *"Don't look at
them, look at Me. Don't be moved by their words, be moved by
what I say over you!"*

Chapter Nine

WOMEN OF VALOR

"What of Jael? Did she have to use a tent peg to kill her enemy? Couldn't she just have turned him over to the authorities while he slept? Possibly, but she didn't. God was okay with her choice, and a song was composed to declare her valor."
—LISA BEVERE, *Lioness Arising*

We recently visited Horseshoe Bend in Arizona. If you have never been there, it is truly spectacular—second only to the Grand Canyon itself in my opinion. Standing on the steep cliff some 4,000 feet above sea level is both fearsome and breathtaking. It overlooks Horseshoe Bend where the turquoise and green reflections of the Colorado River wrap around the horseshoe thousands of feet below. As I approached the guardrails at the edge of the viewing area, I could feel my knees beginning to go weak. Even with the guardrail standing between me and the sharp drop below me, I didn't stay there long, quickly backing myself away to a more comfortable viewing distance. I'm not entirely afraid of heights; I love going to the tops of mountains, lookouts, and buildings, and I love looking out the windows of a plane. However, if you were to put me at the edge of a steep cliff face with nothing standing between us, like a number of the cliffs at Horseshoe Bend, I'm not going to stay there. You'll find me swiftly retreating toward the safety of flat ground. I watched in shock and horror as some of my fellow tourists stupidly (in my view) meandered as close as they could get to the edge of the cliff, all for a photo opportunity. No thanks, not for me. I don't need my feet dangling over any edge for a social media post; I'm happy to take photos of the landscape from a secure distance.

I think of that harsh, steep cliff face when I think of Jael, for *Jael* comes from the root Hebrew verb *yael,* which means "to profit, to ascend." Her name means "a mountain goat." Not just any kind of mountain goat, either—her name can also mean "a wild mountain goat" or, literally, an ibex. A study of the ibex reveals an incredibly sure-footed mountain goat in an otherwise deadly terrain. She can scale precarious heights in search of food and water, all the while evading her predators as she ascends far out of reach of danger. Even her babies are taught within days of birth to follow their mother up and down death-defying rocky passageways. The ibex makes it appear easy to maneuver around the edge of a cliff, far unlike my display of shaky knees.

When watching a documentary on these phenomenal creatures, the commentator remarked, "For many young animals, a wise mother can mean the difference between life and death." I found that intriguing given the famous line of Deborah's song, "I arose, a mother." Could the Lord be prophetically pointing to a company of women who, in an age of precarious and dangerous terrain for our children, are not afraid to wisely lead them through the rocky cliff faces, navigating the paths before them, showing them where to step, how to find their footing, where to get their food (the Word), and how to climb out of range of their predators? I believe so. Another thing the commentator said that caught my attention was, "Up here, your footing needs to be firm, and a head for heights is essential."

Ascend the Heights

While the thought of standing on the edge of a cliff sends shivers down my spine, I cannot deny that there is a calling deep within all of us to climb the highest of heights with the Lord. In the book of Song of Songs, Solomon writes a poetic illustration in which the Bridegroom Jesus is inviting His bride—you and me—to climb with Him to these heights. He says in Song of Songs 4:8 (TPT):

> *Now you are ready, my bride, to come with me as we climb the highest peaks together. Come with me through the archway of trust. We will look down from the crest of the glistening mounts and from the summit of our sublime sanctuary, from the lion's den and the leopard's lair.*

The words used for "come with me," spoken twice in this verse, are two separate Hebrew words. The first is *bo*, and it means "to enter into, to advance, to attack" (Strong's H935). The second is the Hebrew word *eth*, and it means "to enter into, come close to, be near and together to" (Strong's H854). Given these definitions, this verse reads, "Now you are ready, My bride, to enter into, advance, and attack with me as we climb the highest peaks together. Be near to Me as, together, we go through the archway of trust." *The Passion Translation* translates the original words "the crest of Amana" into "the archway of trust." *Amana* comes from one of the Hebrew words for "faith." It can also be translated to mean "a place of security." This beautiful verse paints the picture of you walking with Jesus in oneness and closeness with Him. Through faith in Him and where He is guiding you, He leads you to traverse the rocky cliff faces into a place of security.

Then we read, "*We will look down from the crest of the glistening mounts and from the summit of our sublime sanctuary.*" The New King James version translates this portion of the verse like this: "*Look from the top of Amana, from the top of Senir and Hermon, from the lions' dens, from the mountains of the leopards.*"

The Hebrew word for *look* is the word *shur*; it means "to watch stealthily, to lie in wait" (Strong's H7789). This verse strategically tells us, prophetically, where we will be positioned when we are following Jesus as He navigates us through difficult terrain, "from the top of Senir and Hermon." *Senir* means "breastplate" or "coat of mail," which illustrates your heart being covered from the flaming arrows that are flying through in this age. *Hermon* has a myriad of intriguing definitions. It means "sacred mountain," "mountain of snow" (pointing to the cleansing Blood of Jesus), "high mountain" and "fishing for people." That last definition is gripping. Let's paraphrase the latter part of this verse with these definitions added. No, I am not adding to scripture—I am merely wanting you to see the full picture of what Solomon wrote here through the definitions of the very words he used, so bear with me as I paraphrase for the sake of full clarity:

"Watch stealthily and lie in wait with Me from the top of the mountain of faith, from the heights. You will have a coat of armor, and on My sacred mountain, the mountain of My Blood, a high mountain, we will together fish for people from the lions' dens and the mountains of leopards" (paraphrased).

I wholeheartedly believe that God is anointing a company of daughters in this hour to climb with Him in faith, like Jael, to trust the steps He guides you in so that you can climb the high places. You will be covered as you go, safe in a place of security, hidden from the enemy's eyes. There you will watch in stealth, fully alert and fully awake to his plans. From the safety of this secure place, you will fish for people, rescuing them by the Blood of the Lamb out of the snare of the enemy's lair. Jael is the picture of you, daughter. She reads as an invitation to come out and enter into this archway of trust and faith. Sometimes, that can look like blind faith, especially when all you can see is just the step right in front of you. It can feel precarious and even dangerous at times to follow Him without knowing what's ahead, but you can be assured of this, daughter, that where He leads you will lead to safety and promise. The mantle of Deborah requires of us a surrender to go where He leads, to embrace the unknown, the unpopular paths, and trust that He has made your steps surefooted for the hour at hand.

The Mantle That Covers

When Jael went out to greet Sisera, we read how she asked him to turn aside to her before inviting him into her tent. I want us to read this verse again for additional context. "Jael went out to meet Sisera and said to him, *"Come, my lord, come right in. Don't be afraid.' So he entered her tent, and she covered him with a blanket"* (Judges 4:18 NIV). It's worth noting here that her actions and even words in this moment could be viewed as sexually suggestive. Inviting a lone man into one's tent doesn't exactly depict innocence. However, upon reading multitudes of commentaries on this story, I came across an intriguing point of view. One commentary noted that Jael's actions were far from sexually suggestive, but rather were motherly. Given that Jael's husband and King Jabin were at peace, the two households were familiar with one another; therefore, they were also familiar with Sisera. Sisera's response to Jael is not that of a man looking for a casual one-night stand, but rather a man looking for motherly comfort. She covers him with a blanket and tucks him into bed with a glass of milk, or so he thinks. It's more of a probable conclusion, then, that Sisera considered Jael to be a "motherly" type figure in his life. This is profound when considering our motherly response to today's giants. Another commentary writes this: "When the outside world of national battles comes into her domestic space, Yael takes up a domestic 'weapon of opportunity' and becomes a heroine."[1]

That line strikes me. Consider for a moment how the outside world of warring issues is now entering into our domestic spaces. We have outside forces attempting to govern our children and raise them according to their standards.

The Salt That Preserves

If you're reading this book, it's likely that you are driven by the truth of God's Word. In fact, if you have gotten this far without tossing it aside in offense and anger, then I have no doubt in my mind—we could be good friends. If you're like me, then, you probably get a little riled up when you see lies spreading, particularly when waged against our children. It's because God has given you a divine instinct and hunger for His truth. This mantle is a mantle of righteous justice—not social justice. The two are glaringly opposite. Righteous justice seeks justice according to God's Word. Social justice seeks justice according to man's ideas. With that said, there's a little-known fact about Jael. Her mountain-goat namesake is also a seeker of the truth of sorts—well, at least, the mountain goat seeks out salt. In fact, the mountain goat cannot survive without salt. Why is this important? Grab my hand; I'm about to take you on another little rabbit trail—or, should I say, "Holy Spirit trail."

In biblical times, salt was used to preserve meats and food. This following excerpt is taken from Christianity.com:

Recognize that for many years salt was used as an instrument to reduce the corruption of meat and other foods so that they could be edible for a longer period. Christians who obey God and do his will, serve as a preservative of the human race and the earth by slowing down the moral and spiritual decay of the world around them.[2]

When true believers mix into themselves things like false doctrines, they lose their purity. This will eventually lead to their spiritual lives being worthless and hollow. It's always been an interesting thing to me how Lot's infamous wife "looked back." When the Lord gave Lot and his family explicit instructions to look forward and not look back on the burning cities of Sodom and Gomorrah, Lot's wife couldn't help herself. It showed that the affections of her heart were set on the world, and in doing so she became a dead, ineffective pillar of salt—salt that had lost its taste, which Jesus speaks of in Matthew 5:13 (NLT):

> *You are the salt of the earth. But what good is salt if it has lost its flavor? Can you make it salty again? It will be thrown out and trampled underfoot as worthless.*

Jesus wasn't talking about condiments for food; He was talking about preservation. When a follower of Christ turns and sets their affections on the world, they become, sadly, like Lot's wife—a pillar of salt. Interesting to look at, but nothing of substance. Jesus Himself gave this stern warning in regard to this very concept. He simply and profoundly stated, *"Remember Lot's wife!"* (Luke 17:32 NIV). He then went on to say, *"Whoever tries to keep their life will lose it, and whoever loses their life will preserve it"* (Luke 17:33 NIV). Notice He mentioned the word *preserve* here again. The salt of the Word of God preserves our own lives first—but it does come with a cost. We must first lay down all of our affections for the world, and sometimes that can mean the need to be loved and adored by others. The world and those who have given themselves to mixture—mixtures of truth and half lies, compromise with the scriptures—they will hate you for it. The salt of the Word then preserves the world from moral decay. When sprinkled, it is like salt on a wound—painful to receive, but healing.

Sadly, we have a lot of mixture in the Body of Christ whereby salt has lost its taste. *We* have presumed (and used a "measure" of scripture to affirm this belief) that to be the love of Jesus to the world we must be accepted by them. That is neither the true love of Jesus nor the true Gospel. That's worldly acceptance. Every single time the people began to "accept" Jesus, He confronted them with uncomfortable truths. He was sprinkling salt upon them to see whether they would accept Him or reject Him. Almost every single time, they hated Him for it. Why? Jesus was not interested in the comfort of their opinions; He was after their hearts. He knew that if He catered to their comforts and what they deemed acceptable and loving, then He would have to compromise for them in every single one of their man-made ideologies. Am I saying that Jesus was not loving? Absolutely not. What I am saying is, His version of love and truth does not and never will look like the compromising versions of love and truth in the world.

If we are bowing to what is culturally acceptable, we are bowing to these very demonic ideologies cleverly disguised by the serpent himself, and in doing so we are leading an entire generation to hell, all in the name of love. That sounds harsh, I know, but what's worse? Saying and doing nothing and thinking that I'm loving my neighbor by hiding behind my walls of cultural acceptance in a time of delusion and fear? No thanks. Right now, the world needs the salt of Christ in you to be shaken over these ideologies, giants, high places, and enemies of thought. The world needs the likes of those who will stand up and say, "My generation is being led to hell by a mixture of truth, by ideologies and meditations (the meaning of Sisera's name), and I won't stand for it. I am here to be the salt and the light. I would prefer that your mind is offended, even for a moment, in order that your heart may see the light."

Considering the mountain goat and her need for salt, it is such an incredible analogy that God has written here within Jael. The mountain goat's drive for salt leads her to the mountain peaks—ironically, the very place she needs to be to wage war against the lion's den and the leopard's lair. Jael is the salt that instinctually lures the predator, Sisera, to follow her to the highest peaks. Like the predator that he is, he follows, not realizing the dangers that await him there, but ah, Jael is well-versed on these rocky crags. She knows the cost, and her desire for righteous justice awakens the lion of God within her. It is the hammer of His Word—the salt—that drives down the nail. Daughter, if your drive for truth and righteous justice has led you here, don't mix your salt with the world—keep it pure in the Word and sprinkle it over every social wound you can find, for it is the salt that heals, which our world and our future generations so desperately need.

Acclimated to the Heights

As Jael led Sisera into her tent, she was leading him into unfamiliar terrain, like the mountain goat leading its predator into the rocky heights. Why her tent, though? Why not take him out into the field or behind the oak tree, for example? It is, I believe, because the tent is symbolic of the habitation of God, the meeting place with His presence. The word used for *tent* here is the same word used to describe the Tabernacle—*ohel,* meaning "habitation and dwelling place, the presence of God, a covering" (Strong's H168). While I recognize that the very presence of God only dwelt in the Tabernacle in Deborah's day, Jael's tent is a foreshadow of our own tents where we have now become living tabernacles of the presence of God. Where our tents speak of God's presence, Jael's speaks of her history with God, her relationship with Him. Jael strategically led Sisera here because intimacy with God was positioned in the heights, and Sisera was not acclimated to this terrain.

You might be familiar with the sporting phrase "home-team advantage." The home-team advantage describes a phenomenon whereby the team wins in well over 50 percent of games played at home, as opposed to below 50 percent of games played abroad, where they are in unfamiliar territory. Why is this? The crowds certainly play a huge role in seeing their team cross the finish line in victory; however, I would like to propose that there is another element at play here and it's *acclimation*. Home teams are acclimated to their field, their crowds, and their home, as opposed to a visiting team that is in unfamiliar territory. Little details like not being in the comfort of their own bed at night, different food in different regions, and the unfamiliar crowds and field all contribute to not being acclimated. Therefore, they are caught off guard when facing a strategic battle.

From a different perspective, Jael was acclimated to the heights. A mountain climber whose dream is to climb Mount Everest must get acclimated upon each ascent of their journey. Each new height they reach requires a new level of breathing and seeing. In the same way, we see through Jael's location that she was in constant "migration" with the Lord, moving where He moved and becoming acclimated to that new atmosphere.

When Sisera moved into her tent, Jael had the home-team advantage. Sisera couldn't anticipate what was coming because his guard was down in unfamiliar territory. In the same way, daughter, when you are engaged in battle, bring the enemy to you—don't go down to him. In other words, don't stoop to his level. Lure him to the heights, the high places of God, a place that will bring confusion and frustration to his plans.

Above the Snake Line

A while ago, I heard this interesting term and found that there is a certain altitude where snakes do not go, which scientists call the snake line. This snake line is a place of elevation above sea level that snakes cannot go to, and often campers and hunters choose to trek above this line to avoid the dangers of snakebites on the trail. The journey of those carrying the Deborah mantle is a call to the path above the snake line where the snakes and dangerous beasts normally encountered cannot reach them. This is why you are called to a higher vantage point—so that you are victorious over the enemy, free from the warfare and mind battles that take place below the snake line. Maybe, like me, you have found it hard to ascend and live above the noise and constant warfare, but even now I feel the Lord saying to you, "Daughter, don't live down in the place of defeat! Come up higher with Me and walk with Me on the path of victory!"

Let me end with this practical strategy for you to use. If you are facing something or feeling the snakes at your feet—mental warfare, bombarding fear, anxiety—take it with you into the secret place and worship/ascend until your elevation proves too high for the thing that was assailing you. It works every time.

> *And a highway will be there; it will be called the Way of Holiness; it will be for those who walk on that Way. The unclean will not journey on it; wicked fools will not go about on it. No lion will be there, nor any ravenous beast; they will not be found there. But only the redeemed will walk there, and those the Lord has rescued will return. They will enter Zion with singing; everlasting joy will crown their heads. Gladness and joy will overtake them, and sorrow and sighing will flee away* (Isaiah 35:8-10 NIV).

Deborah's Arsenal

Weapon #9: Salt and Light

In a time of so much mixture, diluted salt, and murky light, God has called us to a life of holiness, purity, and truth. It's a life of being uncontaminated and not compromised by culture's standards. There are far too many counterfeit "women's movements" that look the part and sound the part but have traded their salt and light for something else entirely—chasing man-made ideals and values.

That is not the path for you, daughter. Your path takes you on the road less traveled, to the heights where you must pursue the nourishment and strength of the salt. This is a crucial weapon you will need in the days to come.

Your Charge: Choose the Holy Path over the Popular Path

Have you been able to discern the counterfeit from the genuine in this season? Have you seen the rapid increase of culture-mixed standards infiltrating the Church? Has it felt easier at times to either say nothing or just go along with the narratives? How has it felt in your spirit to do that?

In your journal write down three areas of mixture you have seen in the Church in the last few years. How can you be salt in those situations? How can you restore God's truth and values amid these areas of compromise?

On the other hand, if you are unable to distinguish where there has been mixture, your charge is going to look a little different. I want you to make it your daily habit to read through the Gospels and the letters to the churches in the New Testament. As you read the words of Jesus and the letters of the apostles, consider how they handled opposition and cultural relevance. Did they cater to offense or stand in direct opposition to people's offenses? What was Jesus' standard when facing the culture of His day? Did He bow to their ideas to appease their emotions?

Asking questions like this will help you discern what truth is and what is watered-down truth in today's culture. You can write down any thoughts or teaching you see that you have questions over, then find out what the Word of God says about it. Does it hold to God's standard of truth or does it only hold a measure of truth and is, therefore, a mixture?

This task may seem daunting, but it is the one you are called to—to stay to the holy road and not allow the enemy to lure you off course. Stay at the feet of Jesus—which will often lead you up the mountainous rocky paths (notice Jesus often went *up* the mountains in His prayer time). It is the road less traveled, but you will be able to discern the true salt from salt that has lost its taste. Then you will disperse godly wisdom to those around you—leading them, too, upon the narrow road of safety.

Notes

1. Tikva Frymer-Kensky, "Yael: Bible," The Shalvi/Hyman Encyclopedia of Jewish Women, Evaluations of Yael's Actions, June 23, 2021, https://jwa.org/encyclopedia/article/jael-bible.

2. Staff, "What Did Jesus Mean By 'You Are the Salt of the Earth'?" Christianity.com, December 19, 2019, https://www.christianity.com/wiki/bible/what-did -jesus-mean-by-you-are-the-salt-of-the-earth.html.

Chapter Ten

TEAR IT ALL DOWN

"There are moments in history when a door for massive change opens, and great revolutions for good or for evil spring up in the vacuum created by these openings. In these moments key men and women and even entire generations risk everything to become the hinge of history, the pivotal point that determines which way the door will swing."

—Lou Engle

There are giants in this age that God has solely appointed for women to take down. That might sound like a feministic point of view, but hear me when I say it is the furthest thing from worldly feminism. Modern-day feminism has built a foundation upon what appears to be a godly value—that women are to be regarded equal to men in society. While as a mother of three daughters I wholeheartedly agree with that value as it stands alone—that God created women as equal—I cannot adhere to the doctrines that feminism has built a high place upon. Feminism has built a construct of social justice upon a half truth. Since its rise in the sexual revolution of the '60s, feminism preaches to its followers that women can replace men, that masculinity is toxic, and that motherhood is a downfall. I say this all the time—*check the origins*. In other words, find out where an idea was founded. If it is not founded in the Word of God with sound biblical teaching, you likely have for yourself the constructs of a "high place." For example, securing the right for women to vote was surely a good thing, right? Of course, women should be allowed to vote, but feminism did not want to stop there. Feminism wanted to move into every arena and demand sole propriety of every realm. Don't get me wrong, there are issues with men who treat women as objects and abuse them, but feminism has been possibly the most destructive of ideologies because of its deconstruction of the family unit. It has swiftly moved to destroy the foundational fabric of society and has turned many women from their God-given gift as nurturers into destroyers of life.

Just like any other "social justice" issue that finds solutions for injustices apart from God, these movements always veer grossly off the path of their original intent. Women in the feminist movement have placed themselves above God, above man, and above anyone who stands in the path of their whimsical fantasy of "progressivism." Even if that person standing in their path happens to be the surprise of their own unborn child, they will willingly sacrifice that child, and anyone else, in the name of equality and advancement. It's a high place complete with the blood sacrifice of the innocent. It is in direct opposition to the Blood sacrifice of Jesus, who sacrificed Himself for the sins of the world. Feminism, by contrast, sacrifices the blood of the innocent for their own sins.

God created male and female with equal inherent value, yet attempting to establish equality without God does not end in equality—it creates a myriad of darker, more sinister injustices, because justice according to man will always swing the scales beyond balance. Feminism has become a high place that falls desperately short of God's solution for His daughters. Does God value His daughters equally to His sons? Absolutely. Lisa Bevere says it well, "Men and women are equal, but they are not interchangeable. God made them *both* for a reason." God doesn't look upon His daughters with disdain because they are not males; He adores the way He designed His daughters. In the same manner, He treasures the unique design of His sons.

Male and female are complements to one another, not interchangeable between each other. Modern-day feminism would beg to differ and argue that women should be equal to if not above men. Modern-day feminism sees motherhood as a burden rather than a gift. They believe that the option of sacrificing one's child to the god of self is the height of empowerment. Feminists hold up their grotesque banners in the streets touting the "right" to murder their children in the womb. Meanwhile, these are the same feminists who are handing over their positions to transgender biological males in the name of "acceptance" and "progressivism."

The transgender movement has become yet another high place in which men are proclaiming they are females simply because of a "feeling," and vice versa. Womanhood is not a feeling but is appointed at conception, an assignment by God that cannot be interchanged on a whim. What is extremely alarming is not only the rise of feminism, but the destruction of childhood as a result. These progressive movements and high places are swiftly moving with warped ideologies to invade and destroy the family unit that God designed. If fathers and mothers alike don't arise now, society stands at the point of collapse, for we cannot sustain community without God's construct of family. We cannot create legacy without children, and children cannot bear the burden of indoctrination. How can we *bear fruit* if men are pretending to be women, women are killing their offspring, and if not in the womb, giving them over to confusion as adults? The answer cannot be found in this world but in God alone.

I am reminded of this plea spoken by the Lord through David, "*Who will rise up for me against the wicked? Who will take a stand for me against evildoers?*" (Psalm 94:16 NIV). The Lord's solution for the destructive waves that feminism has left upon society is His daughters, clothed in the mantle of Deborah, armed in righteousness and truth. It is His daughters who will tear down this high and lofty place. This will take courage, but if you don't speak, then who will? My friends, we are in a spiritual war. This will take grit and resolve to rise and speak out against the evils of our day. If you don't rise up, then what will it take for you to stand? At what point of evil will you say enough is enough?

We cannot get lost in the fear of man in this hour, for a divisive wedge has been engaged within the Body of Christ, and it is this wedge that says, "If you confront these issues, you are taking sides in politics." Can I just say, *enough* with that lie! The enemy has disempowered a sleeping Church for far too long. The mantle of Deborah is governmental, and if you are afraid of offending your friends and family by standing in the truth because of the fear of "politics," I'm not going to lie—this battle will take you out. You're going to have to decide to shake off that fear now and realize that this is a moment to which you have been called. At the end of the day, are you pleasing God or man?

That is a question that drives me. Am I more concerned with what my friend thinks than what God has called me to say? Deborah was not afraid to engage in the politics of her day; she charged forward, unafraid. She and Barak together forcefully opposed the king, the government of their day. Notice it was man and woman together. Imagine what would be said of Deborah and even Barak if they lived in our time. "They are too conservative. They shouldn't be engaging in politics; that's not what the Church is meant to do. Deborah isn't loving enough. She should be praying for her enemies rather than fighting against them. Barak shouldn't be slaying anyone; how evil of him. Deborah's opposition to the king does not represent Jesus. Deborah is a woman; she should stay silent. Deborah is too divisive." Need I go on? Sound familiar?

Daughter, I pray you would rise in the courage and the strength of His might. If you are confused by the narratives of our day and where you should stand, find out their origins and then test them against the Word of God. If an origin is founded by man and upon a lie, then you have every right to stand in the truth of the Word and call it down. One surefire way to tell if an origin is a high place or not, is to ask this question: "Is the world in agreement with this idea?" If you are aligning with ideas and concepts that are largely accepted by the world, I can almost certainly tell you that is an idea that is not accepted by God. It might have a glimmer of truth to it, but it is a half-truth. Look for the lie, for you will always find it. Don't associate with half-truths; plant yourself in inherent truths. One way to tell if you are called to tear down a particular high place is to find the lies that irritate you the most. Do you hate the lie of abortion? Do you hate the lies being spread to your children? Once you know what high places you are called to, it will be easier to tear them down. Are you ready to slay some giants?

Truth Offends

Many Christians lose their resolve in the face of offense. For fear of offending someone, they refuse to speak and declare what is true. It has become the mindset of many that to offend is not to love, but that couldn't be further from the truth. Jesus was never concerned with offense—He offended the religious and the unsaved alike merely by speaking truth. In fact, He offended them so much that they nailed Him to the Cross.

However, the Cross was not the only time their offense drove them wild with hate for Him. We find multiple accounts before the Cross in which the crowds lusted to silence Him and even attempted to kill Him. Remember when Jesus fed the five thousand? No sooner had their tummies been filled with hearty bread and delicious fish than they were driven away in offense mere hours later. What did Jesus say to them that was so offensive? "Eat My flesh, drink My Blood."

Of course, it's clear to us now what He meant, because in hindsight you and I know that Jesus was referring to the communion of His Blood, but they didn't know that then. The Jews had a very strong set of rules and regulations—set for them, mind you, by God Himself. Within those rules were strict guidelines for food. So Jesus' statement came across as literal cannibalism. Read this dialogue in John 6:26-42 (NIV) between Jesus and those who had just eaten their fill of the loaves and fishes.

> *Jesus answered, "Very truly I tell you, you are looking for me, not because you saw the signs I performed but because you ate the loaves and had your fill. Do not work for food that spoils, but for food that endures to eternal life, which the Son of Man will give you. For on him God the Father has placed his seal of approval."*
>
> *Then they asked him, "What must we do to do the works God requires?"*
>
> *Jesus answered, "The work of God is this: to believe in the one he has sent."*

So they asked him, "What sign then will you give that we may see it and believe you? What will you do? Our ancestors ate the manna in the wilderness; as it is written: 'He gave them bread from heaven to eat.'"

Jesus said to them, "Very truly I tell you, it is not Moses who has given you the bread from heaven, but it is my Father who gives you the true bread from heaven. For the bread of God is the bread that comes down from heaven and gives life to the world."

"Sir," they said, "always give us this bread."

Then Jesus declared, "I am the bread of life. Whoever comes to me will never go hungry, and whoever believes in me will never be thirsty. But as I told you, you have seen me and still you do not believe. All those the Father gives me will come to me, and whoever comes to me I will never drive away. For I have come down from heaven not to do my will but to do the will of him who sent me. And this is the will of him who sent me, that I shall lose none of all those he has given me, but raise them up at the last day. For my Father's will is that everyone who looks to the Son and believes in him shall have eternal life, and I will raise them up at the last day."

At this the Jews there began to grumble about him because he said, "I am the bread that came down

*from heaven." They said, "Is this not Jesus, the
son of Joseph, whose father and mother we know?
How can he now say, 'I came down from heaven'?"*

What was Jesus doing here? Why was He not concerned with losing followers? Unlike many ministries, churches, and even pastors today—who would rather share messages that tickle the ears than lose followers on social media or congregation members—Jesus wasn't concerned with a loss of followers. He was marking out the territory of the New Covenant that He was building, territory that would come through His own Blood poured out on the Cross. Notice He said "very truly" twice. In Greek, that word is *amen* (Strong's G281). You may not know it, but every time you say *amen*, you are expressing and affirming your acknowledgement of the truth. You are saying, in essence, "*Yes, yes*, this is true." *Amen* in Greek means "most assured truth, certain truth, so let it be, very"—which is "truly, confidently in truth." Jesus was affirming truth, and it was the truth that drove away many of the disciples who had just witnessed the miracle of the feeding of the five thousand— and whose tummies were still filled with said miracle.

This is an hour when we cannot be more concerned with the feelings of people, which flow and ebb as quickly as the tide, than with pleasing the Lord by establishing His truth. It is not a lie or a half-truth that is going to set our generations free, it is not an idea or a fantasy, it is the whole truth and nothing but the truth. Jesus *is* truth—there is no lie in Him. It is the proclamation of inherent truth in every matter of society that will set the generations free. Not the idea of loving them in delusion.

Jesus said to the Jews who had believed Him, *"If you abide in my word, you are truly my disciples, and you will know the truth, and the truth will set you free"* (John 8:31-32 ESV). Jesus spoke these words not long after the feeding of the five thousand. In fact, between chapters 6 and 8 of John, you will find numerous accounts in the feeding of the five thousand in which Jesus is establishing Himself in truth as the New Covenant and there is a wrestling with the people. His words create division (see John 7:40-42). This is confronting because much of the modern-day, seeker-sensitive church movement is built upon "loving" their congregations. Does that mean we should not be loving people? Absolutely not—of course we are to be driven by the love of Jesus. However, the stark difference is His love does not hide the truth. The love of Jesus does not conceal a lie.

In John 8:31, Jesus knew His time was drawing closer to the Cross, and His words were sharp and telling, laser focused on the mission before Him. I have had many Christians tell me that speaking truth is divisive and I should be more loving. Listen, there is no love in telling a lie, or even in silence. You can say you love all you like, but if your love is not speaking the truth, you are essentially hugging your friends as they fall into the abyss of hell. True love sees the impending danger and warns of it. Today, our generations are being led to the slaughter, literally and spiritually, under the guise of "love." How cunning of the enemy. He has used a virtue of God—love—and convinced a generation to fall into hell by that name. See the half-truth there? This is where many fall short of understanding what is truly happening in our society. They, like Adam and Eve, have been lured in by the question, "Did God actually say…?" God never said that speaking truth was hating your neighbor; in fact, hiding the truth is the very epitome of hate.

The Weapons of the Word

By today's standards, Deborah's, Barak's, and especially Jael's actions would have been perceived as hateful, divisive, and unloving. Jael was about to carry out a justice that would be considered highly offensive in our day. Am I suggesting we need to do something like her? It needs to be said loud and clear that I am not condoning physical violence of any sort, especially the kind we are about to read from Jael. Hers was a truly brutal and gruesome move. However, there are spiritual lessons we can draw from her actions.

Imagine for a moment how the larger Body of Christ might respond to the news of what she did. Jael would be cast out into the shadows, canceled, never to be spoken of again. It's important that we understand the context of the times and learn how to decipher the differing strategies of warfare according to the age we now live in. Under the Old Covenant, God's people had to fight in hand-to-hand combat because their battle was still with flesh and blood. Through the New Covenant of Jesus, the battle lines have shifted, and our warfare is now largely a battle with spiritual principalities. God's people were still at war with spiritual principalities then, but they had no supernatural weapons by the Blood of the Lamb to fight with. We do. Therefore, while ours is a spiritual fight, there are significant spiritual lessons within Jael's physical warfare that we can apply to the battles of our age today. There are three strategic tools that Jael used to take down Sisera.

1. *The Mantle*

*And he turned aside to her into the tent; and she
covered him with a mantle* (Judges 4:18 BST).

When Sisera first entered Jael's tent, she covered him with
a mantle. Why is this important? Do you remember what
Sisera's name means? Meditations. This represents the battlefield of the mind, where thoughts and ideologies build their
high places above God. This mantle she covered him with prophetically points to the Deborah mantle that God has anointed
you to carry today. She covered the meditations of the mind
with the truth of God's Word. The word used for *covered* is
the Hebrew word *kasha,* and it means to literally "cover over,
make a covering, conceal, and overwhelm" (Strong's H3680).
God is anointing you in this hour, daughter, to cover and overwhelm the lies with the mantle of Deborah, which is the truth
of the Word of God.

It reminds me of the quote by St. Augustine, *"The truth is
like a lion, you don't have to defend it, let it loose, it will defend
itself."* Unfortunately, far too many within the Body of Christ
are hesitant to let the truth loose; therefore, they are giving lies
free jurisdiction to reign. We must cover over and overwhelm
the lies with the inherent truth.

2. *The Milk*

*"I'm thirsty," he said. "Please give me some water."
She opened a skin of milk, gave him a drink, and
covered him up* (Judges 4:19 NIV).

Why did she give him milk? And what could milk possibly mean for us today during the intense warfare we face? It seems kind of counter-productive, does it not? Milk in scripture represents God's Word for the spiritually immature. Peter described milk as a drink for the spiritually young:

> *Therefore, rid yourselves of all malice and all*
> *deceit, hypocrisy, envy, and slander of every kind.*
> *Like newborn babies, crave pure spiritual milk,*
> *so that by it you may grow up in your salvation,*
> *now that you have tasted that the Lord is good* (1
> Peter 2:1-3 NIV).

So why did Jael give Sisera milk? It speaks of sharing the truth in a relatable way for those who are spiritually immature. We need to convey deep messages with simplicity. The Gospel need not be over-complicated, but we must simply and profoundly speak the truth so that those who are willing to let go of all malice, deceit, hypocrisy, envy, and slander will be freed of the meditations of the principality of Sisera and be able to drink the pure Gospel and be filled to contentment like a newborn baby.

By contrast, for those who refuse to adhere to truth—the milk of the Word of God—the Word of truth will cause them to get sleepy, much like a newborn, and they will be lulled into their own deceit. Which is exactly what we see happen to Sisera. He was lulled into a state of "milk drunkenness," blinded to perceive God's next move. When we witnessed the downfall of Roe v. Wade, no one could have predicted that this almost 50-year contract with death would be brought down under the most pro-death administration in America's history. This reminds me of the principality of Sisera—they were lulled into a state of delusion by their own pride, believing that by their own power they could reinstate this death decree. Instead, the simple, inherent truth that God values the pre-born child in the womb was the very milk that blinded them and continues to. At exactly 10:10 am a decree went out to all the land —a stone into the head of this giant. John 10:10 (AMP) says; *"The thief comes only in order to steal and kill and destroy. I came that they may have and enjoy life, and have it in abundance (to the full, till it overflows)."* Could it be any clearer that God's word prevailed over this lie. His declaration rippled out to the Nations as he declared, *"choose life, that thou and thy seed may live."* (Deuteronomy 30:19, KJV)

How do we minister the milk of the Word today? By speaking the constant, simple, profound, biblical truths of the Word of God to a lost and waning generation. By sharing "Jesus loves you and died for you" loudly and clearly from every conceivable vantage point that we have. By declaring His value for every human being. By speaking the unadulterated, guileless, and undeceitful Word of truth. By refusing to mix this pure milk with the meditations of our day. The pure milk of the Word will draw in those whose hearts are truly thirsty for the truth, and it will set them free.

Paul speaks of the milk of the Word in Hebrews:

> *In fact, though by this time you ought to be teachers, you need someone to teach you the elementary truths of God's word all over again. You*

need milk, not solid food! Anyone who lives on milk, being still an infant, is not acquainted with the teaching about righteousness. But solid food is for the mature, who by constant use have trained themselves to distinguish good from evil (Hebrews 5:12-14 NIV).

You will know the spiritually mature, as opposed to the spiritually immature, because they are able to distinguish good from evil. If a leader in the Body of Christ cannot rightly discern what is good and what is true, you have good standing to ask whether that person is leading you and others into the whole truth and in righteousness. There should be serious red flags if someone you follow is unable to distinguish and call out what is wrong and what is evil, because it reveals that they have not graduated from the elementary milk of the Gospel. They are failing to constantly use and train themselves in the solid food of the Word. If they are still drinking baby milk, why are you giving them authority to lead you spiritually? Either they have blatantly ignored the pure milk for the sake of crowd pleasing or they have turned aside from the truth. Be very wary of any leader—whether a worship leader, a biblical teacher, a pastor, or even a social media influencer—who refuses to acknowledge and call out the elementary truths of God's Word, who cannot clearly discern simple right from wrong according to scripture. When Jael offered Sisera milk, it was both a mockery of his inability to discern truth and a trap to lull him into a state of fatigue. Do not fear speaking the truth of the Word, for it will blind and therefore expose those who have chosen to be influenced by the principality of Sisera.

It will awaken others to the reality of the truth, which will lead them into repentance and, therefore, freedom.

3. The Hammer and the Tent Peg

> But when Sisera fell asleep from exhaustion, Jael quietly crept up to him with a hammer and tent peg in her hand. Then she drove the tent peg through his temple and into the ground, and so he died (Judges 4:21 NLT).

I cannot over-exaggerate the sheer boldness of Jael in this moment except to merely say Jael is savage. Nothing here describes hesitancy, only calculated accuracy for the task God had set before her. Why did she quietly creep up on Sisera, though? The hammer and the tent peg both represent, you guessed it, the Word of God. *Sisera* can also mean "binding in chains" and speaks of strongholds and attitudes of the mind. In this very moment, Jael used a prophetic picture of the Word of God and tore down the altar of his high place in the very position where it had been built—the mind. She drove it through his temple, where our warfare is positioned today, where high places are built today. She drove the Word into the high place and tore down in a moment the idolatrous high place of Sisera.

The word used for *drove* is the Hebrew word *taqa*, and it means "to blow, to trumpet, to blast" (Strong's H8628). It speaks of violently driving the weapon deep into the meditations of the high place that Sisera had built. The tent peg represents the establishment of territory. Isaiah 54:2 (AMP) says:

*Enlarge the site of your tent [to make room for more
children]; stretch out the curtains of your dwell-
ings, do not spare them; lengthen your tent ropes
and make your pegs (stakes) firm [in the ground].*

This is governmental; this is territorial. When we read
Jesus declaring the truth, He was enlarging the site of His
tent. He was stretching out the habitation of His dwelling to
inhabit the New Covenant that He was building by His
Blood. He was tearing down the old to make room for the
new. It was offensive, but it had to be done. Likewise, Jael
established new territory by driving the tent peg, by the
hammer, down into the ground through Sisera's temple. She
was tearing down the old to make room for the new. It is time
that you and I grab hold of our hammers and our tent pegs
and do the same.

Right then, Barak had been pursuing Sisera. In Judges 4:22
(NIV) we read:

Just then Barak came by in pursuit of Sisera, and Jael went out to meet him. "Come," she said, "I will show you the man you're looking for." So he went in with her, and there lay Sisera with the tent peg through his temple—dead.

Our Spiritual Weaponry

What caused Jael to kill Sisera in such a gruesome way? I believe the Lord positioned her as a prophetic foreshadow for you and me. Where her battle was physical, ours is supernatural. God instructed her to kill her enemy in the way that she did so that you and I would have a blueprint of how we are meant to handle the enemy through the spiritual weapons He has given us in our day. We've already read from 2 Corinthians 10; however, I want to revisit it again in light of Jael and drive the peg in a little deeper (pun intended).

For though we live in the world, we do not wage war as the world does. The weapons we fight with are not the weapons of the world. On the contrary, they have divine power to demolish strongholds. We demolish arguments and every pretension that sets itself up against the knowledge of God, and we take captive every thought to make it obedient to Christ. And we will be ready to punish every act of disobedience, once your obedience is complete (2 Corinthians 10:3-6 NIV).

So what are the weapons of our warfare in the spirit? We know that the Word of God is our weapon. The scriptures aren't just telling a nice story: *"The word of God is alive and active. Sharper than any double-edged sword"* (Hebrews 4:12 NIV). The Blood of Jesus is our weapon. Communion is our weapon. When we face these principalities, high places, and strongholds in our day, we have the power and the authority to tear them down by the Blood of the Lamb.

When I shared this principle in my previous book, I received a testimony some months later from a woman who read it. She told of how she took the Blood of Jesus and prayed it over her children's school. Every day, when she would drop her children off at school, she would march out at the front fence and plead His Blood before going home. She would declare promises of protection in the Word, like Psalm 91, and declare that no plan or assignment of the enemy could come near her children or their school. Within weeks of doing this, an active shooter approached her child's school at midday, armed with multiple guns. His intent was to go on a killing spree. However, something caused him to freeze right at the entrance, at the very gate where she had been praying. Because he froze, security guards spotted him in time and tackled him to the ground.

She sent me articles and shared her amazement at how God had moved on her behalf as a direct result of her authoritative prayers. When you know your authority, the enemy can't stop you. When you are declaring the Word of God; you are driving that hammer and tent peg deep into the ground and establishing your territory; you're smashing a mighty blow through the high places and strongholds of our day. The weapons we fight with are not natural, but they are supernatural.

Notice in the 2 Corinthians verses that it says, "*We demolish arguments and every pretension that sets itself up against the knowledge of God.*" This is the grounds of our warfare today. Arguments and pretensions are the high places of our day. The Greek word used for *arguments* is *logismos,* and it means "a reasoning, a thought, conception, an idea" (Strong's G3053). "Pretension" is the Greek word *hupsoma,* and it means "a height that is lifted up, a lofty thing" (Strong's G5313). Do you see it? The "wind words" we are encountering on every front, the confusion of thoughts and speech, the ideologies that are taking the world captive are *all* high places.

How do we discern the difference between a high place of the enemy and a high place of God? Look for the ideas and concepts that set themselves against God and the foundations He created. For example, the high place of abortion sets itself against the creation of God—the baby in the womb— by saying that the pre-born baby is not human or is a parasite that must be removed. We tear down the high places by exposing them to the truth of the Word of God. The weapon against this ideology is Psalm 139:13-14 (NIV):

> *For you created my inmost being; you knit me together in my mother's womb. I praise you because I am fearfully and wonderfully made; your works are wonderful, I know that full well.*

Find the lie and expose it to the truth. We tear down these high and lofty thoughts and ideas, we tear down Sisera, by hammering the Word directly through his meditations.

Finally, the scripture tells us to "*take captive every thought to make it obedient to Christ*" (2 Corinthians 10:5 NIV). How do we do that, though? How do you take a thought captive? By subduing, surrounding, and ensnaring it with the truth. Remember how Barak and Deborah were led by God to ensnare Sisera and his armies at the waters of ensnaring? When you speak the truth of His Word over a lie, the Lord will do the rest. He will send out His army of warring angels to fight on your behalf. This principle can be applied for the massive giants you see in culture or any high place or lie that has set itself as a stronghold in your own mind.

Just as Deborah prophesied, God gave this enemy into the hands of a woman. Today, I prophesy there are high places that God has given into the hands of His daughters to tear down. You, daughter, are anointed by Him to carry the mantle of Deborah. By driving the tent peg down with the hammer of the Word directly into and through the meditations and high and lofty thoughts of the world, you will see these ideologies torn down. You are establishing new territory to make room for more children. This is about legacy. I'm not just referring to physical children; I'm referring to the prodigals who will come home as you make room for them under the tent of truth.

Deborah's Arsenal

Weapon #10: Your Hammer of Justice

The enemy often tries to convince you that you are being harsh or unloving when you dare to oppose the injustices around you. Today, however, God is revealing the hammer of justice He has given to you and the anointing and responsibility to wield it over the injustices around you. It's not an option; it is the call of God upon your life, and you have everything you need in your arsenal to release His justice and His solutions to every realm of jurisdiction He has called you to. Don't stand idly by waiting for someone to confront injustice; swing your hammer, mighty daughter, for you are called to this moment.

Your Charge: Confront the Giants in Your Path

Let me ask you again: what giants do you see around you right now? What are you seeing globally or even locally that is defying the righteousness and justice of God? What is agitating you and causing your spirit to grieve?

Write them down in your journal. You may be asking, *"Where do I begin?"* Allow me to encourage you and give you some first steps. First, you are more anointed for this than you know. You are a *giant-killer,* and the enemy is afraid of you knowing this. Let your first step be to simply pray and prophesy against the giants you see. Spend some time in worship and swing your hammer there—then ask the Lord, *"Now what do You want me to do?"* You'll be surprised at the doors and opportunities that open to you as He guides your steps supernaturally and naturally.

A Little Extra Encouragement

Are you battling warring thoughts today? Practice this biblical principle of tearing down the high places. Is your mind at war against itself? Have you been believing lies? Lies like, "I am never going to break free of this habit. When am I ever going to feel free from depression? Will we ever get free of debt? I don't think I'll ever walk in my calling. I'm worried my children will never return to the Lord." If your thoughts are at war within you, it's time to chase after them and ensnare them with the Word. Find out what God says about you. Find out what the Father says about your children. Search out a word in scripture that jumps out at you as your weapon and then *chase* after every thought and capture it with the truth.

Daughter, these are your lions and bears. The lions and bears that David had to fight in the wilderness on his own—we all have them. When you can hunt them down, facing Goliath is going to be no different. The little beasts are no different than the big ones once you know who you are and whose you are. Go hunt down some lions and leopards and come up higher into the realms of His glory where you will only see truth, and then hammer down your tent peg violently into those lofty thoughts that have set themselves against the knowledge of God about you. It's time to tear it all down.

Part Four

THE DEBORAH ARMY

Chapter Eleven

NOT ON MY WATCH

"Have nothing to do with the fruitless deeds of darkness, but rather expose them."
—Ephesians 5:11 NIV

Now that we have the spiritual elements of our battle plan clear, you might be asking, "What should I do in the natural?" The years of 2020 and 2021 were more or less an education on where we as the Body of Christ stand on moral issues. In the wake of the pandemic, these two years erupted into a myriad of other issues. One such issue was the sudden disclosure of sexualized books and curricula that had been covertly introduced into schools. Programs displaying explicit content that even an adult should not be subjected to were being covertly taught to children, without their parents' knowledge or consent, some as young as five. This is where the rubber meets the road, so to speak. Where do we stand as Christians when demon-inspired ideas are being introduced to our innocent children? Do we stand back and hope for the best in fear of what people might say? What if others conclude that you are engaging in the taboo territory of politics by intercepting these ideologies? In his book *Ekklesia*, Ed Silvoso describes engaging in cultural battles as moving "from the pew to the city square." He writes:

> The first-century Ekklesia introduced a radical and revolutionary social agenda that launched a process that literally changed the world. With the subsequent institutionalization of the Church, however, what was a lifestyle that implemented Jesus' agenda became programs of good deeds that fall short of transforming society.[1]

Has the Church reduced our commission of "go into all the world" merely to a number of programs of good deeds? Have we failed to implement the vital, transformative power of the Gospel into every realm of society? Why are we more largely concerned with church programs that benefit the church alone, rather than engaging in social issues that benefit the communities around us? We were never meant to be islands unto ourselves. The Church of Acts illustrates to us how we are meant to engage in the culture around us, not hide from it. Ed goes on to write:

> It is most unfortunate that when the split between liberal and conservative believers

took place in the last century, the liberals kept the social agenda and the conservatives kept the Scriptures, generally speaking. This resulted in one stream speaking up for social justice, without an accompanying emphasis on a personal relationship with God through Jesus Christ, and the other stream being very Bible centered, particularly when it comes to the point of being born again, yet being dismissive of the social aspects of the Gospel for fear of the so-called social gospel. These two streams ended up opposing rather than complementing each other.

The key is in embracing a position where we are Word-based on ethics and Spirit-empowered on social issues. In fact, the New Testament Ekklesia modeled this very well.

The teachings of Jesus that the first-century Ekklesia modeled constitute what is now known as Christian ethics. No other philosophy has come close to matching it. In fact, the modern world is built on it because Christian values and ethics have no rival in either the secular or the religious arena.

There are four major social evils that the Ekklesia tackled successfully: systemic poverty, slavery, female servitude and the degradation of the family.[2]

Could it be that the modern-day Body of Christ has failed to engage in the issues of our day for fear of coming across as "too political"? When Jesus instructed us to pray, "Thy Kingdom come, thy will be done, on earth as it is in heaven," He wasn't handing you a pretty little prayer wrapped in a lovely pink bow. No. He was handing you a spiritual weapon with governmental authority—an assignment to pray and inject His divine perspective and solutions into every social degradation. God designed government, so why are far too many Christians viewing this as the one area of society that we should not be involved in?

When you see these issues raise themselves against His true knowledge, you have been given the power by His Blood to overturn and overthrow principalities and thoughts of darkness and wickedness. The issues we face today are very much the same as the first-century Church, they just come under some different names in our era—poverty, human trafficking, feminism, and the decay of the family unit through abortion, the waning desire for Christ-centered marriage between a man and a woman, not to mention the perverted agenda to sexualize our children. The list goes on. But could it be that God is raising up a remnant, bold in their stand for truth, fierce in their opposition to evil, immovable in their stance on the Word of God, and courageous in their tenacity to hammer the truth into every lie? I believe that you, daughter, are a part of this remnant army that the Lord is raising in this hour.

One final thought from Ed Silvoso: "Jesus' Ekklesia...is a spiritual entity vested with governmental jurisdiction on earth to change world systems for the better."[3]

Hammering the Peg of Truth

When parents began to see the exposure of these destructive and sexually explicit books and curricula that had been stealthily introduced into their children's schools, they began rising up en masse, opposing school boards and calling them to account.

I want to introduce you to a new friend of mine, Alicia Farrant, a mother of five who lives in Florida with her husband of 21 years, she is a daughter of God that truly carries this mantle of Deborah. I came across her story in late 2021, where she had sent me an Instagram reel that she had compiled of the battles she had been facing up until that point, in her children's school during the pandemic years. She had been reading my previous book, *Releasing Prophetic Solutions,* and as a mother of five, God began revealing to her the true power of her combined prayers and action. At this time, mask mandates were a prominent thing in public schools, and many parents were becoming increasingly concerned with the mental ramifications of restricting their children's breathing and faces. I'm not about to make this a more contentious book than it already is, but when vast disparities are occurring with government officials proclaiming these restrictions, and they happen to be the very ones not adhering to their own rules, we, as parents and as children of God, have every reason to question unlawful and restrictive mandates set by ungodly governments. Earthly government, according to Gods design, is created to serve the people, not the other way around. "I arose, a mother" is more than a statement, it's a call to action on every front, including in the realm of government as we operate from a higher Kingly authority and our mandate from heaven is to be applying the Father's Kingdom to policies, laws and regulations. After all, it's not up to the world to decipher morality, it's up to us. Jesus did not give His authority to the world itself, He gave it to His disciples, and the question is, what have we been doing with it? For many years, we've been floundering within the walls of the Church, too afraid to engage in the culture outside, too concerned that we'll appear unloving for opposing evil. Not anymore. There is a wave of righteous courage and boldness that is arising in the hearts of His sons and daughters, and I strongly believe His daughters are keys to accelerating His Kingdom upon the earth.

Alicia recognized that the restrictive mask mandates for her children at school were deeply affecting their mental health, so she rose into bold action. She had come across a quote on social media that read, "it just takes one match to start a fire." And then in the caption of that quote, it read, "If you haven't been to a school board meeting, what are you waiting for? Who are you waiting for? Are you waiting for somebody else to rise up? It is you who needs to rise up!" (Author unknown.) Alicia told me, "I felt like the Holy Spirit was saying, "Now it's your time. You need to rise up. You need to be the voice." It's moments like these where I have often found the enemy can war at us the loudest, right as we stand on the threshold of a heaven-ordained moment of destiny, he whispers, "Who do you think you are? Your voice won't have any impact; what can one person like you do?" I want to encourage you, resist those lies with everything you have. Instead of retreating, Alicia rose up and wrote a simple invitation on a local Facebook forum inviting other parents to come along to the school board meeting, and join her. At their first meeting, just five parents appeared alongside her, and together they confronted the school board and let them know that they felt their voices were not being heard.

By the time the next school board meeting came around, their number grew from just five parents to 20 parents. Together, they again made their voices heard and were met with silence from the board as the board continued on with their agenda. Within a matter of two or three more meetings, their number grew to over a hundred parents showing up. At this point, the board members shut the doors to the meeting and refused to let them all in, but by now the momentum had shifted as frustrated parents grew all the more louder and bolder, and relentlessly continued to fight together until they were heard and saw the mandates fall. What Alicia may not have realized in this moment, was that this battle was like the lion and the bear that David fought in the wilderness, and her Goliath was waiting just around the corner.

In October of 2021, a message was sent out in a "moms for liberty" group that Alicia was a part of, alerting other mothers to begin checking their schools for a particular list of books that had unknowingly been introduced into school curriculums and libraries. Books that were explicitly depicting pornographic illustrations suggesting sexual and homosexual activity that children could experiment with. To her horror, sure enough, these very books, containing pornography, homosexuality, pedophilia, and molestation, were in her children's school library and approved by the school board members. Enraged, Alicia and her husband marched down to yet another board meeting and listened on while a friend read one of the books over the microphone to the board. The board flew into a panic and had their friend removed by security for reading "inappropriate content," yet, they were the very ones who had deemed this content appropriate for 14- to 18-year-olds. Here were the board members, adults themselves, in a room full of adults, offended by the very material they had approved for children, refusing to address or remove it.

By January of 2022, the fight continued as the board remained staunch against their demands, refusing to address the explicit material in the school curriculums and libraries that Alicia and the parents kept finding. It was at this point, that the Holy Spirit began to prompt Alicia to run for school board and unseat one of the members there, to be a voice for righteousness in place of their evil agendas. Her and her husband prayed, and both of them felt that this was the direction of the Lord for her. So, she positioned herself to run. She arose, a mother. I watched on and prayed for her as I would see her sharing updates of her hammering in her election signs around her neighborhood, attending meetings, and raising awareness of what was happening. I so admired how a mother of five was fighting relentlessly, rain, hail, or shine, for righteousness in the culture that her children were growing up in. In the midst of this, Alicia was invited to attend the historical signing of a law by the name of HB 1467, a legislation that demanded that school boards and districts MUST show complete transparency to parents with their selection of materials that are provided to the children. This legislation removed the dictator-type style of authority that boards had previously depended upon, that allowed them the right to deny parents a say in what their children had access to and were being taught. This legislation became a contentious piece of law, aggressively opposed by far left agendas, however, it prevailed. Florida's governor, Ron DeSantis, had said at the signing, "In Florida, our parents have every right to be involved in their child's education. We are not going to let politicians deny parents the right to know what is being taught in our schools. I'm proud to sign this legislation that ensures curriculum transparency." Alicia was present for the signing of this bill and was further invited by the governor to speak there.

Her battle to win a school board seat continued, and she faced a relentless onslaught of accusations and character assassination; however, she continued, knowing that it was God who was fighting alongside her. Every step of the way, she faced demonic opposition, but she continued to put one foot in front of the other, and fight for her children, fight for her region, and uphold righteousness in the battle. In October of 2022, Alicia won the battle and was elected as a school board member for her district, replacing one of those who had been a voice for darkness. Now Alicia is seated as a voice for righteousness in her children's school district. God honored Alicia for her fight, and He elevated her voice in ways she could never have imagined, having her speak at the signing of righteous legislation, speaking before millions, and then, seating her in a position of governmental authority over her children's school district and region. This, my friends, is the mantle of Deborah at work. This is how God anoints His daughters, how He carries them through the fire of fierce battles and brings them out the other side with victory. This doesn't mean that everything will be easy from here on out. Alicia still has battles to fight as she is the lone voice of righteousness in a sea of wolves; however, if God is for her, who dare stand against her?! As she recently shared with me, she had a dream where she was casting out demons and she woke up speaking in tongues. Though the voice of the accuser may attempt to continue to intimidate her in her new position of authority, God is continually affirming her that in her position she is anointed to cast out the demons that surround her. We are in a time where, I believe, we are going to see mass deliverance over people and over regions. God has positioned Alicia as His strategic weapon to be a part of this deliverance of regions.

My question to you, daughter, is this: What are you waiting for? Where has God positioned you? You may be a lone voice, but the Lord can cast your voice out, like a stone upon the waters, and send out ripples of His righteousness that will awaken the hearts of others to stand up in bold courage. Your voice has a ripple effect. What are you waiting for? God is waiting on you. Deborah knew this; she knew that if she didn't stand up, who would? Notice in Judges 5:7 (NIV) it says;

> *Villagers in Israel would not fight; they held back*
> *until I, Deborah, arose, until I arose, a mother*
> *in Israel.*

Deborah had to recognize that unless she stood up, no one else would. Daughter, unless you stand up, no one else will.

You are anointed for this hour; just as Alicia stepped into the mantle of Deborah, so must you.

I love her story because Alicia perfectly illustrates this partnership in the natural with what God says in the spiritual. Our battle may be a spiritual one, but there are natural and earthly actions we must partner with in faith. Alicia didn't just pray and hope for the best—she prayed and she fought. She prayed and she spoke. She prayed and she opposed. She prayed and she established new territory. She prayed and she drove the hammer down. She prayed and she moved to offer divine solutions by running as a school board member.

What is it that the Lord is waiting for you to move into by faith? What is it that you can engage in to declare His Kingdom in an area of degradation in your society? Is it in politics? Then rise up and don't be afraid. Is it in the area of poverty in your region? Then ask the Lord what you can do to offer divine solutions. Is it in an area of injustice? Then begin moving to engage in the issue. It doesn't have to be massive gestures at first; it can simply be putting one foot in front of the other. Just like Alicia who, through a two-minute speech to her board, removed the high place that had been set up over her children's education. Follow the voice of the Holy Spirit, for He will lead you to take the next step. As small as it may seem, walk it in faith, knowing that He goes before you and has made a way for you.

Hold Fast to the Testimony of Jesus

We are in a war of the ages. It's not like any war before us. Have you ever noticed how sand in an hourglass appears to quicken as it draws close to the last remaining seconds? We are likewise in a moment of quickening as we approach the coming of our Lord. This means the enemy knows that his time is short, and therefore his assault has grown violent as he rages in a last-ditch attempt to establish his throne above the Lord's. In Revelation 12:17, we are told that in the last hours, *"And the Dragon raged against the woman and went to make war with the remnant of her Seed, these who keep the commandments of God and have the testimony of Yeshua"* (Aramaic Bible in Plain English).

If there was ever any question about the hour in which we live, that verse makes it plainly clear. The war against women, the war against our seed, is because the enemy knows his time is extremely short. He rages because he is well aware that women are a great threat in this hour. He knows that the seed they bear—children and legacy, both spiritual and physical— pose extreme danger to his rule of darkness. Why? Have you ever considered the names of the generations alive today? As I write, the generation that is being birthed in this hour is called Generation Alpha. Before them, Generation Z. Together, these generations speak of the Alpha and the Omega. They speak of the last and the first, the beginning and the end. Is it any wonder, then, that up until now it is these two genera-tions that are targeted by the enemy perhaps more than any generations before them? Why? They have been anointed by God to be conduits of the last and greatest outpouring of the Holy Spirit that the world has ever seen. While I am not suggesting that they will be the only conduits of outpouring, I believe they play a strategic and key role in what the Holy

Spirit is about to pour out. We as mothers are anointed with the mantle of Deborah. We are gatekeepers of this outpouring, and we too will bear witness to what the Lord is about to do. However, we cannot relax our guard in this moment of intense warfare and opposition. What is our weapon of the hour? Revelation 12:17 tells us it is the testimony of Jesus. Revelation 12:11 (NIV) also confirms this:

> *They triumphed over him by the blood of the Lamb and by the word of their testimony; they did not love their lives so much as to shrink from death.*

The Greek word used for *testimony* is the word *marturia* (Strong's G3141). This is a legal term, speaking of giving sound witness in a court trial. It literally means "to give witness to, to testify against." It is speaking of a witness standing on trial before a courtroom, declaring what they have seen and known to be true. This testimony of what we know to be true, found in Jesus—who *is* the Word (see John 1:1)—is our weapon to triumph over the enemy. By declaring truth over every single lie, we are hammering into the temple of the enemy the testimony of Jesus. This word, *marturia*, is mentioned throughout the New Testament in constant reference to speaking what is right and what is true. In Paul's letter to Titus, he writes speaking of correcting false teachers:

> *For there are many rebellious people, full of meaningless talk and deception, especially those of the circumcision group. They must be silenced, because they are disrupting whole households by teaching things they ought not to teach—and that*

for the sake of dishonest gain. One of Crete's own prophets has said it: "Cretans are always liars, evil brutes, lazy gluttons." This saying is true. Therefore rebuke them sharply, so that they will be sound in the faith and will pay no attention to Jewish myths or to the merely human commands of those who reject the truth. To the pure, all things are pure, but to those who are corrupted and do not believe, nothing is pure. In fact, both their minds and consciences are corrupted. They claim to know God, but by their actions they deny him. They are detestable, disobedient and unfit for doing anything good (Titus 1:10-16 NIV).

Not everyone who says they are for Jesus is willing to speak His testimony of pure, undefiled truth. May we hold fast to the truth in this hour, for it is evidently clear that in the last days many will fall away from Him for the fear of man, for being more concerned with what people think than what God says.

Just to be clear, I don't say this to condemn anyone for being afraid of stepping out. I think it's normal to wrestle with our voice as we learn to use it, but the final frontier in the heart of man is the fear of man and a test we all have to endure in our journey to being a Deborah for the times. Do you feel that wrestle often? How do you overcome it? Have you yet to push through the torrent of opinions and judgments? Here's a small key before we move on—pray for the fear of the Lord to encompass you, but don't blame me for what happens next. When the fear of the Lord falls on you, the fear of man leaves, and what has been bottled up inside you comes out with force.

Here Comes the Remnant

In part of Deborah's song, she sings these governmental words:

> *Then down marched the remnant of the noble;*
> *the people of the Lord marched down for me*
> *against the mighty* (Judges 5:13 ESV).

The word for *marched* is *radah* in Hebrew. It means "to have dominion, to rule, to dominate" (Strong's H7287). This can also mean "to subjugate, to tread down, to reign over, prevail against." This speaks of God's daughters marching against these ideologies, acutely hearing His voice, and speaking forth His voice over these deceptive high places of our day—those that may appear strong and mighty. I am reminded of Elijah in this verse; after having killed and defeated the prophets of Baal, the voice of Jezebel sent Elijah into isolation from her intimidation. Hiding away in a cave, he cried out to the Lord, *"I alone am left"* (1 Kings 19:10 NKJV), but the Lord gently reminded Him, *"Yet I have reserved seven thousand in Israel, all whose knees have not bowed to Baal, and every mouth that has not kissed him"* (1 Kings 19:18 NKJV).

Perhaps you have been feeling a little like Elijah—alone in this fight. I am here to remind you today that you are far from alone. God has reserved a remnant of His daughters who refuse to bow down to the idols of our day. A remnant of daughters whose mouths will not touch these ungodly ideologies.

Daughter, God has reserved you as His remnant. There is a remnant arising in this hour—a company of daughters bearing the mantle of Deborah, set apart for God's glory. A remnant who refuse to bow to the narratives of our day. They will tear down every high place, they will break down every wall, for they are on a rescue mission of the ages—to bring the prodigals home and make way for the King of Glory.

Pick Up Your Keys

Imagine being at a car dealership and a brand-new car is driven to where you are and left running with the keys inside. The salesman looks over at you staring and says, "It's been paid in full, enjoy!" What would you do? Would you hop in the car and drive away? Or would you think it was a trick and walk away?

Unfortunately, too many of God's daughters have walked away from the vehicle (the ministry, mantle, and mission) God has given them and forfeited the keys (the authority, power, and anointing) that operate it. Instead, many have resorted to a powerless life of wishing and hoping that one day they will be able to be used in a powerful way when that moment is now!

Your testimony is more powerful than you think it is, and the anointing and mantle upon your life is begging to be used to smash the most impossible obstacles around you. So let this be your charge—pick up your keys today, daughter, take your authority, and step into your shoes in Jesus' name!

Deborah's Arsenal

Weapon #11: The Fear of the Lord

We are living in a time when the fear of man has increased to a suffocating level with the introduction of demonic narratives and ideologies that have employed political correctness and cancel culture to enforce their regime. It's easier to just go along with the flow, not to rock the boat, and bend to the fear of man—but doing so would be in direct disobedience to God.

Daughter, in these times your weapon is the fear of the Lord. Psalm 111:10 (NIV) says, *"The fear of the Lord is the beginning of wisdom,"* and it will counteract the fear man tries to put on you. The fear of the Lord is not the kind of fear that satan and the world projects; this a reverential respect for the Lord. The word used for *fear* in Psalm 111:10 is *yirah* and it can mean "awesome, extreme, fearful reverence" (Strong's H3374). These definitions illustrate to us that we are to live with an extreme reverence of God. We are to be on guard with every step we take, everything we take in, everything we speak, and everyone we listen to.

This kind of reverence leads to wisdom, and divine wisdom is something we desperately need in this age. Only with godly wisdom can we rightly discern what is right and true in this age of mixture and confusion. So today, take off the mantle of the fear of man and put on the fear of the Lord! Choose every step with reverence to God and He will make your path straight before you.

The Charge: Live as a Testimony

Do you wrestle with the fear of man? Do you feel the pressure to conform and stay silent?

Write down some of the fears you have of what people might do to you if you were to stand up. Now rip that page out of your journal and throw it in the trash—openly giving those fears to Jesus and acknowledging Him as the one and only Lord of your life.

Daughter, you were called to be a witness of Jesus and your life is a broadcast of His goodness. Sometimes that will mean speaking when no one else is speaking. Sometimes that will mean others will mock you in the public square (or, today, our social media squares). Sometimes that will mean you are spat on for your faith. At the end of the day, know this—your reward in heaven is great. Don't underestimate the potency of being a testimony because God will use you in ways you could never have expected. Share what God has done and is doing in your life, and boldly testify against the lies of this age. Go in courage, for God has gone before you and Jesus stands with you.

Notes

1. Ed Silvoso, *Ekklesia* (Bloomington, MN: Chosen Books, 2017), 139.
2. Ibid., 139-140.
3. Ibid., 140.

Chapter Twelve

A ROARING COMPANY OF DAUGHTERS

The Lord gives the word; the women who announce the news are a great host: "The kings of the armies—they flee, they flee!" The women at home divide the spoil.
—Psalm 68:11-12 ESV

The War on Your Voice

Have you been feeling as though there has been a war against your voice? Is it this sense of intimidation that overwhelms you every time you speak? It might be what people have said or how you feel—this trepidation to stand up and speak out. Has it felt as though there has been a muzzle and a gag order over your mouth whenever you go to step out in faith? If this resonates with you, know that you are certainly not alone. There has been an all-out assault against the daughters of God to silence those who are speaking truth and to intimidate those who are ushering in the sound of His purity.

When I was a little girl, I loved to watch the movie *The Little Mermaid*. It was one of my favorites as a child, along with *The Lion King*. I was always terrified, however, of Ursula. I would anticipate her scenes, knowing when she was about to come on screen, and I would run up to our video player and press the fast-forward button until I skipped past the segments with her. If, by the way, you have no idea what I am referring to with the video player, it means you missed out on the wonderful experience that was the VCR. I kid, I kid—but seriously, the VCR was truly an experience. You couldn't just jump ahead to a scene at the touch of a remote-controlled button. You had to physically get up off the couch and sit with eyes glued on the screen as you held your finger on either the rewind or fast-forward buttons and agonizingly waited for the scene you wanted. It was a true art form to get to that scene without going too far past it. Rented movies from Blockbuster weren't often rewound to the beginning either, which meant waiting for your movie to rewind—this was all part of the experience. Then, there were the pre-movie advertisements. Movie time was a whole ordeal, but I digress.

As I was praying over the contents of this chapter, I couldn't move from the allegory of *The Little Mermaid*. I believe the Holy Spirit was bringing this fictional tale (see what I did there) to mind for a profound reason. The name *Ariel* is a Hebrew name, and it means "lion of God." The name *Ursula*, on the other hand, is of Latin origin and it is derived from the word *ursa,* which means "little she-bear." I know the phrase "mama bear" comes to mind at the mention of a bear; we associate fierce mothers with bears for a reason. However, in a biblical context, bears relate to strongholds and powerful demonic forces.

In the context of the battles we face in our day, I believe Ursula is a picture of the principality of Jezebel. In fact, I have had multiple dreams and visions of this stronghold principality, Jezebel, and every time the Lord has shown me an image of Ursula, an octopus-like creature with many arms. Let's hit pause for a moment, because you might be asking, "Are you telling me that God endorses Disney?" Allow me to be perfectly clear: absolutely and profoundly *no.* Their agenda has become clear, particularly in recent days. However, let me just say that the Holy Spirit uses pictures that are common or familiar to us to convey and help us understand what we are dealing with. Through these parabolic pictures, He often helps us to understand how to overcome these principalities.

For example, I was recently praying for the child of a loved one who was experiencing demonic oppression. My friend was doing everything they knew to see their child free, but to no avail. As I was praying, I asked the Lord to expose anything that was hidden, and then I went into an open-eyed vision where I saw a green demon spirit surrounding this girl. It looked like a dark entity I had seen on a movie flyer somewhere, but I could not place my finger on it. That night, a friend shared on their social media an image of a movie they were watching, and right there, front and center, was the exact same green figure as the one I had seen in the vision. It was called "the green goblin." Now, why would God use a picture from a movie like that? When I looked it up, I found a key hidden in the narrative of this fictional creature. The writer of this comic had said that the green goblin gained and increased its power by way of exposure and agreement. I immediately knew why the Lord showed me this demon in this way. He was highlighting to me that there had been an open door of exposure that needed to be closed. This demon was accessing my loved one's daughter and surrounding her with oppression because of this open door.

When I told my friend, she immediately knew what door was open through connection with certain friends online and through movies. She abruptly closed those open doors in the natural and in the spirit, and I instructed her to pray over the house afresh, anointing the doors and entryways, particularly her daughter's room, with anointing oil. Within days, we began to see immediate results. Her daughter began to break free of the oppressive thoughts and of her own accord, for the first time, started to request godly counsel.

Notice that the spirit entered through entertainment. Pay attention to what you are allowing enter into your home. The Holy Spirit uses allegory today just as Jesus used allegory and parabolic stories to articulate intricate spiritual truths in an easily digestible way. I encourage you, pay attention to the things He highlights to you. You will know it's from Him because it will align with His Word and will give you instruction and strategy. Just as He highlighted strategy to me through this one vision that brought about a significant breakthrough, so too is He longing to speak to you. He is looking for a company of daughters to release His divine solutions through, to break down the spiritual strongholds around families and in the culture around you.

With all that in mind, let us come back to Jezebel. I have seen this principality look identical to Ursula, as an octopus witch with many arms. You might be asking, "How does the principality of Jezebel relate to Deborah, though?" Deborah was not only a judge, but she was also a prophetess (see Judges 4:4), which positioned her to partner with the Spirit of God for strategic solutions for her people. While it would take me a whole new book to teach on the principality of Jezebel, I'll briefly bring to your attention some main fruits of the principality of Jezebel that you can be aware of. She seeks to silence and intimidate the pure and prophetic voice of the Lord (see 1 Kings 19:1-3). She usurps territory, authority, legacy, and inheritance (see 1 Kings 21). She attempts to surround you with confusion and strife so that she can assassinate your divine assignment. She tries to overthrow the true voice of the prophets and will often send false prophets (think of Ursula's two slimy eels) of her own to undermine what God is actually speaking. All of these "fruits" are the arms of her strength, and she gains continued strength through our agreement with fear, intimidation, insecurity, and compromise. You can easily spot someone inflicted by the ink of her tentacles, because they will never adhere to or acknowledge the entire truth of the Gospel—they will be rife with compromise.

Jezebel, like Ursula, seeks out the prophetic voice of God through His people and seeks to either silence, intimidate, or annihilate them. In the movie *The Little Mermaid*, Ursula preyed on young Ariel in her state of confusion. Do you notice the parallel with what is happening to our youth today? A state of confusion has descended upon the generations to destroy and confuse their identity, with the end goal of stealing their voice. Ursula offered the little mermaid a deal: she would give Ariel that which she most desired—a change in her identity— for the sound of her voice. Ursula longed for Ariel's voice, just as Jezebel longs to usurp the voice of the lion of God, but it is one thing she can never have. This principality has descended upon the generations of today with an ink cloud of murky confusion to disorient our youth and our children. Her biggest threat? The pure daughters of God, for they drown out her every lie and cut off her every arm. She desperately seeks to stop God's daughters, mantled with the anointing of Deborah, from ever realizing their true identity and the power of their voice.

This is why, daughter, you have likely experienced this sense of muzzling. Whether you have been grappling with the confusion of who you are or what you are called to, or whether it has simply been this "ink stain" of fear over your voice every time you speak out. Maybe you have even noticed those close to you have been infected by her voice, seeking to silence you as you speak out. This does not mean we are to demonize our friends and loved ones. We disempower the effects of Jezebel by choosing to forgive and bless those who persecute us and continuing in our mission of declaring the purity of God's truth. In *The Little Mermaid*, Ariel needed her father the king to intervene in her situation, to reinstate her voice. In real life, we need the voice of our Father to be louder than any voice around us.

This brings us back to the beginning of this book in Chapter One. Whose voice are you listening to? Have you been muzzled by the voice of this octopus-like demonic witch, or are you rehearsing what the Father has said over you? If you're going to overcome this principality, which certainly wars over the mantle of Deborah, you are going to need to find your roar—the sound of the lion of God in you. If you haven't found your roar yet and only can utter a mere whisper, allow me to encourage you to dig into the scriptures and discover what the Father has said about you. Then, speak these promises out louder and louder every day until you feel His roar growling upon the chords of your own voice. Then, let Him out. Let Him roar. This may take you shouting down a room on your own one night or, like I have done many a time, going to war in my car as I drive. (Don't worry, I pull over first.) This roar may come through tears as the Holy Spirit breaks down the lies and cuts off the strangling arms of Jezebel's grip. Either way, let Him roar over you, in you, and *through* you. It is His roar that will strengthen you to be able to hold this mantle with ease. Otherwise, I won't lie to you, the mantle that is meant to be a gift will feel more like a heavy burden if you are trying to fight off Jezebel's lies on your own.

When Nate and I had to follow the voice of God by going to America at the beginning of the pandemic, in the midst of all the fear and intimidation that surrounded us with the noise and confusion, we soon discovered God's plans in the midst of it all. God used the closed door of our borders back in Australia to allow us time to birth our third daughter in the United States. We had not planned for her, but God had. Ava Arielle was born in the midst of political and pandemic upheaval. Her name, *Ava*, means "voice, breath, sound" and *Arielle*, a variation of Ariel, means "lion of God." Together, her name means "voice of the lion of God." We knew that her birth in America was not only significant for her individually but also for us, as her parents, as a spiritual legacy and authority over both our home nation of Australia and now the United States too. She was born on 1/11/21, and when I looked up verses correlating with her birth date I was amazed to find they all spoke of legacy and inheritance. Ephesians 1:11, for example: *"In him we have obtained an inheritance, having been predestined according to the purpose of him who works all things according to the counsel of his will"* (ESV). It's just like God to birth a seed of legacy and hope during chaos, for He works all things together for our good. He is longing to do the same through you. It may be a physical child He has planned for you or a spiritual birthing of the new—either way, when you follow His voice expect legacy to follow.

I find it almost comedic that Ursula's name means "little she-bear," because you may remember the meaning of Deborah's name. *Deborah* literally means "a bee." I believe that God is anointing His daughters in this moment to move as a host of bees to protect the hive, which is the family, and the pure honey, which is His Word and His prophetic decrees. God is anointing you, daughter, to arise and attack this imposter principality as one. It is time for His daughters to arise and swarm on this little she-bear that has been attempting to rob the hive. God is anointing us, as mothers, to take her down once and for all.

Don't Tolerate Her

In his book *Unmasking the Jezebel Spirit,* the late John Paul Jackson wrote, "Tolerance becomes the cultural buzzword meant to disarm anyone who embraces biblical absolutes."[1] And in another quote, he wrote, "People who are deceived by lawlessness do not understand that by rejecting God's laws they are led into even greater licentiousness and enslavement to sin. When lawlessness is practiced, it becomes easier to do it again. Thus, lawlessness leads to more lawlessness."[2]

Here are two more fruits of Jezebel—the deception of tolerating evil for the sake of appearing good. Tolerance itself leads to lawlessness. Tolerance has become a worldly virtue and, as such, is paraded around in self-righteousness by those who unknowingly embrace the teachings of Jezebel. Sadly, far too many of the world's inhabitants have been stung by this ideology, and what's even more tragic is that we within the Body of Christ have a great number of fellow brothers and sisters who are voicing these poisonous and treacherous lies.

In Revelation, Jesus writes to the seven churches, each representing Christ's Church as it stands today. His letter to Thyatira in particular is compelling as it speaks into the issues we are indeed facing on a global scale today and also within the Church. He writes in Revelation 2:18-29 (NIV):

> *To the angel of the church in Thyatira write:*
>
> *These are the words of the Son of God, whose eyes are like blazing fire and whose feet are like burnished bronze. I know your deeds, your love*

and faith, your service and perseverance, and that you are now doing more than you did at first.

Nevertheless, I have this against you: You tolerate that woman Jezebel, who calls herself a prophet. By her teaching she misleads my servants into sexual immorality and the eating of food sacrificed to idols. I have given her time to repent of her immorality, but she is unwilling. So I will cast her on a bed of suffering, and I will make those who commit adultery with her suffer intensely, unless they repent of her ways. I will strike her children dead. Then all the churches will know that I am he who searches hearts and minds, and I will repay each of you according to your deeds.

Now I say to the rest of you in Thyatira, to you who do not hold to her teaching and have not learned Satan's so-called deep secrets, "I will not impose any other burden on you, except to hold on to what you have until I come."

To the one who is victorious and does my will to the end, I will give authority over the nations— that one "will rule them with an iron scepter and will dash them to pieces like pottery"—just as I have received authority from my Father. I will also give that one the morning star. Whoever has ears, let them hear what the Spirit says to the churches.

The name of the church, *Thyatira*, means "a castle, a perfume, and a sacrifice of labor." Jesus acknowledged the work of the Church; however, His words are striking and fearsome when you consider how many within the Bride have compromised their stand for Him by tolerating Jezebel. The word Jesus used for *tolerate* in this text is the Greek word *aphiémi*. It means "to send away, to leave alone, to permit" (Strong's Greek 863). It comes from the two Greek words: *apó*, which literally means "away from," and *hiēmi*—"to send." Interestingly, the *NAS Exhaustive Concordance* uses these additional definitions to describe this word, *aphiémi*: "abandon, allow, divorce, forgive, give permission to, leave, neglected, permit, yield."

Jesus has strong words to those of us who permit and allow the works of Jezebel. Wouldn't "forgiving" sins be a good thing, though? It's interesting that one of the definitions is also "divorce," which speaks of a complete separation—not in the sense of separating oneself in consecration, but in the sense of separating oneself from the awareness of Jezebel's evil works. This paints the picture of a Christian burying their head in the sand like an ostrich and utterly ignoring her works of darkness. What does this do? Gives her voice and gives permission to her to continue in the evils she commits.

When Roe v. Wade fell, I was utterly dismayed at the response of many church leaders who quickly buried their heads in the sand, abandoned the conversation, and allowed the permission of evil ideologies to continue by refusing to outwardly oppose abortion and celebrate the severing of this death decree over the nation. In fact, I had pastors write to me privately and tell me that my celebration of the end of this abominable death decree that has sacrificed millions of babies upon the altars of Jezebel was, in their view, "unloving and unkind."

Listen, there is nothing loving and kind about neglecting the truth, for it is the truth that sets people free. *"So Jesus said to the Jews who had believed him, 'If you abide in my word, you are truly my disciples, and you will know the truth, and the truth will set you free'"* (John 8:31-32 ESV). We must put an end to this mindset in which we are complicit with evil for the sake of keeping up appearances. Do we love truth more? Or do we have a higher value and regard for our appearance and how people perceive us? We can love those in darkness without agreeing with their works. Deborah did not comply with evil; she fiercely and aggressively opposed it. Something that would have been considered as unloving and unkind in our world today, but she was not concerned with how she appeared to man. She was a woman after God's heart anointed to take down the giants of her day.

Daughter, we overcome the principality of Jezebel and every other demonic force by the Blood of the Lamb and the word of our testimony. *"They triumphed over him by the blood of the Lamb and by the word of their testimony; they did not love their lives so much as to shrink from death"* (Revelation 12:11 NIV). Notice that this verse highlights how they did not love their lives so much as to shrink from death. They weren't intimidated by what man says or what man may threaten. They continued to march forth in truth and in righteousness. A remnant is rising in this hour—a remnant of daughters, unafraid of the mighty battle, fierce in their resolve, with eyes unflinching. Their gaze is fixed on Jesus, the Author and the Finisher of their faith. Here they come—daughters marching down against the mighty.

Then down marched the remnant of the noble;
the people of the Lord marched down for me
against the mighty (Judges 5:13 ESV).

The Lion Is Roaring: "My Daughters Are Rising!"

The Holy Spirit has been burning this phrase into my spirit, "My daughters are rising." These words have been consuming my heart like a battle cry and I can feel the fiery passion of a loving and protective Father calling out to His daughters, "It is your time to arise." I can sense the compassion in His tone for those who have endured much, but I can also sense the urgency in His decree, "It is time to arise, mighty daughters. I am picking you up out of the ashes; it is time to shake off the dust." The Holy Spirit led me to these verses in Zechariah 9 that spoke deeply to me:

> *Then I will camp around My house [as a guard]*
> *because of an army, because of him who passes by*
> *and returns; and no oppressor will again over-*
> *run them (Israel), for now My eyes are upon them*
> *[providentially protecting them]* (Zechariah 9:8
> AMP).

As I read this verse, I saw in a vision a picture of one like a disfigured lion with no teeth chasing the daughters of God in relentless pursuit. I saw the King's daughters being chased by this mangled and toothless lion into a desert wasteland. He was seeking to devour them and they were running in fear of

239

him, though he had no ability to bite. They had been running a long time and were exhausted and weary as they dragged their feet across the hot desert sands. Tired with no fight left in them, they were seeking shelter in hidden caves. I could see that there were vast numbers of the King's daughters in this desert, but they had been separated and isolated, each to their own cave, shivering in corners and huddled up in fetal positions. They looked battle-weary with mud and blood covering their faces from their long pursuit. I saw again the one that appeared like a disfigured lion and he was now pacing back and forth out in front of their caves, roaring fiercely as he patrolled the entrances where they hid. I saw the King's daughters cowering in intimidation as they peered outside their caves in fear of this enemy. Within the vision, I became indignantly angry; a righteous anger arose within me as I watched this unjust scene unfolding. I cried out, *"God arise! Let His enemies be scattered!"*

The True Lion Emerges

At that moment, a mighty rushing wind picked up from within the desert, and there within the wind I saw the true Lion emerge. His eyes were blazing like hot coals of fire and His very presence commanded a shift in the atmosphere with unspoken authority. He began to walk toward the caves where His daughters were hiding, and as each powerful paw hit the ground, a quaking could be felt across the desert sands. I watched as the one like a disfigured lion began to growl and grow nervous as the true Lion approached. The wind continued to surround the true Lion, and it began to spread to every cave where the daughters were dwelling. Within the wind, a voice came to each daughter in hiding: "This is not who you are. Arise." At that moment, the true Lion lifted up His head and released a mighty, thunderous roar that split the air in two. I saw the sky itself split into two, and suddenly it was as though the daughters' eyes were opened. Before, they could only see a mutilated but intimidating lion chasing and surrounding them, but the roar of the true Lion revealed the scene for what it really was. As the sky split, his identity was revealed as a defeated and cowering foe, and they could now see clearly that he was toothless and much smaller than he at first appeared. The daughters arose as the wind rushed over them and released within them a renewed strength and fight. One by one, they began to emerge from their caves, looking upon the horizon where their King Lion stood. With His glorious mane flowing majestically in the wind, He called out to them, "Come, daughters, arise. Take the swords before you and defeat this notorious counterfeit lion, for today I have given you the victory."

As the King's daughters looked down, they realized at the foot of their caves lay a weapon—a sword. They picked up the sword and began to shout in triumph as they ran out of their caves in vast numbers and pursued the enemy until he could no longer be seen.

As this incredible vision ended, I began to read with tears streaming down my face what follows on from Zechariah 9:8:

> *Rejoice greatly, O Daughter of Zion! Shout aloud, O Daughter of Jerusalem! Behold, your King (Messianic King) is coming to you; He is*

righteous and endowed with salvation, humble and unassuming [in submission to the will of the Father] and riding on a donkey, upon a colt, the foal of a donkey. I will cut off the [war] chariot from Ephraim and the [war] horse from Jerusalem, and the bow of war will be cut off. And He will speak [words of] peace to the nations, and His dominion shall be from sea to sea [absolutely endless], and from the River [Euphrates] to the ends of the earth. As for you also, because of the blood of My covenant with you [My chosen people, the covenant that was sealed with blood] I have freed your prisoners from the waterless pit. Return to the strong-hold [of security and prosperity], O prisoners who have the hope; even today I am declaring that I will restore double [your former prosper-ity] to you [as firstborn among nations]. For I will bend Judah as My bow, I will fit the bow with Ephraim [as My arrow]. And I will stir up your sons, O Zion, against your sons, O Greece, And will make you [Israel] like the sword of a warrior (Zechariah 9:9-13 AMP).

Come Out of Hiding

I believe the word of the Lord in this hour for His daughters is found in these very verses. Where many of you have found yourselves in relentless warfare, oppressed and hiding away in caves of a waterless pit, Jesus your King Lion is releasing a deep and prolonged roar over you today. He is calling you out of the cave that has held you captive and in fear. He is revealing the true identity of the deceitful, toothless lion, and He is reminding you of the weapons that you carry. He is awakening the warrior-daughter within, for He has given you all the power and authority in heaven and on the earth. He is decreeing with an ear-splitting and resounding roar:

> Awake, awake oh daughter of Zion. Arise with the mantle of Deborah! Come out of hiding. Shake off the ashes. Look around and see that I have made you victorious, oh beautiful one! Rejoice greatly, shout aloud! For I am here. I am your victory. I have called you as a reformer. I have made you like the sword of a warrior. You are My mighty weapon.

You Are Called to Take Down the Giants of the Land

He is your providential protection, He is the Lord strong and mighty in battle, and He has given you victory over your enemy this day. Now pursue what has pursued you. Take back the captive children who have been enslaved by the enemy's tyrant rule. I see multitudes of daughters awakening as they read this word, and I see them running in relentless pursuit of what has tried to consume them. I see that the Father has given them keys and strategies to disarm and dismantle the enemy's oppression. I see longstanding strongholds breaking as they strike the enemy with the brutal force of their God-given authority.

I see the King's daughters marching into a fresh and new governmental authority in this specific moment in time. Where their voices have been silenced or oppressed for generations, they will be instrumental in ushering in this long-awaited, mighty move of God that is beginning to sweep across the earth. They will march hand in hand with their men, and together they will see cities restored. God is raising up His daughters in strength and in unequalled numbers in this hour, for the enemy has once again blinded the daughters of the earth in a newfound oppression of feminism. However, God's daughters will move in unrivalled supernatural power, marching to heaven's beat of justice and purity, daughters of the Cross consumed with the love of their King. They will together see giants fall and nations surrender to the glory of Jesus.

Deborahs, Arise

I can hear the gates of hell shrieking at the sound of this approaching army—they cannot stop what is coming. Here they come; can you hear them? God's daughters of Zion, a mighty army of beauty and strength. They are coming over the mountains like a mother bear with resolution in her eyes to protect her young, to restore the family, redeem the unborn, retrieve the lost, and bring the prodigals home. They are coming to pour out the sweet fragrance of Jesus into the earth. Here they come—warriors and nurturers, soldiers and protectors. They are fierceness, love, and strength combined.

God is calling to you, dear daughters. A charge to arise as mothers over the land and territory you have been assigned. You are the spiritual protectors, nurturers, and defenders over your families. Village life as we have known it has been ceasing, but watch as God's Deborahs arise. Like a cloak spreading across the nations, this divine calling from heaven is resting upon a generation of daughters; they will courageously and fearlessly push back the darkness and expose it to the light.

> *God Almighty declares the word of the gospel with power, and the warring women of Zion deliver its message* (Psalm 68:11 TPT).
>
> *Now you are ready, my bride, to come with me as we climb the highest peaks together* (Song of Songs 4:8 TPT).

Together we will wage war in the lion's den and the leopard's lair!

I hear the Lord saying in this hour, "Deborah, Deborah, rise up!" There is a breaker anointing in your shout. There is a potency on what God is speaking through His mighty warrior-daughters across the earth in this hour. I see the Lion of Judah both smiling and roaring in fierceness behind you today. Beloved daughters, you are called, purposed, and equipped to slay demonic principalities, restoring His righteousness to the land. He is with you. Now is the time, now is your hour. Take down the giants in the land.

Deborah's Arsenal

Weapon #12: Your Song

Daughters, your greatest arsenal against the enemy's assignment to silence you is to lift up your voice. It's the seasons you feel the most muzzled, stifled, frustrated, and voiceless that you need to lift up your song louder in the face of the onslaught. Jezebel is the antithesis and opposite of Deborah in every single way. Where she silences and attempts to muzzle God's daughters, the mantle of Deborah shows us God's solution for all of His daughters—to release the sound of heaven, the praise of Jesus, and to sing a song of victory unto the Lord. Deborah may have sung after the victory, but you can sing your song of victory before you see the battle is won.

Your Charge: Shatter the Muzzle and Prophesy!

Have you felt muzzled and silenced for most of your life? Have you felt like you have always been undermined? Have you undervalued your own voice because others didn't see the gold within? Has it caused a dormancy of your voice?

In your journal, write down three ways you have felt muzzled recently. What is the enemy afraid of you being a voice for? Take a moment to shatter the assignment against your voice. Place your hands over your mouth in a prophetic act of faith and declare loudly, *"Devil, I will not be silenced anymore. I loose my voice in Jesus' name!"*

Now begin to prophesy over yourself as you hear the Holy Spirit leading you. Listen to what He says and repeat it. Write it down so you don't forget and revisit His words every time the enemy attempts to muzzle you again.

Notes

1. John Paul Jackson, *Unmasking the Jezebel Spirit* (Flower Mound, TX: Streams Creative House, 2002).
2. Ibid.

CONCLUSION

I wanted to finally share this small portion of a prophetic word I wrote and shared on September 18, 2017, about Deborah. As you read the final words in this book—and close its pages—know that the God of Angel Armies is releasing upon you this mantle; He is writing this story upon the very pages of your life. Not to glorify Deborah—or any one woman—but to glorify the name of Jesus in all the earth. This mantle of Deborah is not, after all, about Deborah—it's all about Him. Deborah's mantle is merely a tool that the Father is using to glorify His Son. As His daughters answer the call of this charge, all that will be left and seen is Jesus.

The Charge from Heaven

I hear a loud charge from heaven as the daughters of righteousness are being called upon to unite as an army joining in force. I see the daughters moving in powerful authority—overturning the works of darkness and injustice. There is a movement of daughters—both young and old—who are waking to the dawn of a new day. They are no longer satisfied with the status quo, no longer content to sit behind the scenes, and they are being stirred to the sound of the voice of their beloved King Jesus to move forward and take their place.

The Holy Spirit is breathing courage, strength, and purpose into them as He whispers truth to their spirits: "You are here for a purpose, you have a voice, and you are equipped with My heavenly strategy and resolve. You are My beloved daughter, and you are significant for this very hour. Do not hold back anymore.

Up! For this is the day when the Lord has given Sisera into your hand. Has not the Lord gone out before you? (Judges 4:14 ESV).

The Lord is shouting this over every daughter, "Up! Mighty daughter! Up!" Your King is calling you out from the shadows and calling you into His marvelous light to establish justice and redemption to all generations.

If you take anything away from this book, let it be Judges 4:14 as your charge. May you go and release the name of Jesus, stripping down principalities and declaring His righteousness over all unrighteousness—may you tear down the works of darkness and rebuild the ancient ruins of many generations. May you say as Deborah did, "I arose, a mother!" I want to leave you with one final charge for the days to come. This charge comes from another mantle—Esther's. Like Judges 4:14, this scripture calls every daughter to attention, I leave this with you as you go:

> *For if you remain silent at this time, liberation and rescue will arise for the Jews from another place, and you and your father's house will perish [since you did not help when you had the chance]. And who knows whether you have attained royalty for such a time as this [and for this very purpose]?* (Esther 4:14 AMP)

"Up, mighty daughter. Up!" For such a time as this!

ABOUT CHRISTY JOHNSTON

Christy Johnston is an intercessor, teacher, prophetic voice, and justice carrier. Christy's burning heart for justice and intercession has led her on a life journey of prayer, contending for major world issues. She is passionate to raise and empower God's sons and daughters to release the Kingdom of God across the earth. Together with her husband Nate and their three daughters Charlotte, Sophie, and Ava, they now currently live in Texas, United States and travel back between the U.S and their homeland of Australia regularly, on missions of prayer and prophecy.

NATE & CHRISTY

We see a world where God's sons and daughters are awakened to the truth of who they are in Christ establishing the Kingdom of heaven here on the earth. Our desire is to see God's people permeate the earth with the glory of Jesus.

Everyday Revivalists is our ministry, because our mission is to raise up everyday revivalists in every sphere of influence through our online courses, our prophetic words, and anything else we might offer—we're in this to make a difference in your life. To help you know your identity in Christ, be founded in love and walk in your royal authority.

www.nateandchristy.co

From

CHRISTY JOHNSTON

Access Heaven's Solutions For Every Problem and Crisis That You Face in Life!

The mystery of the Kingdom is that, through our prophetic prayers and decrees, we can partner with God to change our world.

Seasoned prophetic intercessor, Christy Johnston, shares the revelation she received when God intervened in her life by revealing supernatural strategies to the struggles she was facing. As Christy partnered with what God was showing her, she was emboldened to pray in another dimension—a realm of Kingdom authority that sees answered prayers and circumstances shift. You have access to this realm!

Watch God transform your world as you partner with Him in prophetic prayer!

Purchase your copy wherever books are sold.

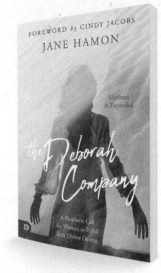